Critters of Colorado

Pocket Guide to Animals in Your State

ALEX TROUTMAN

produced in cooperation with
Wildlife Forever

About Wildlife Forever

Wildlife Forever works to conserve America's outdoor heritage through conservation education, preservation of habitat, and scientific management of fish and wildlife. Wildlife Forever is a 501c3 nonprofit organization dedicated to restoring habitat and teaching the next generation about conservation. Become a member and learn more about innovative programs like the Art of Conservation®, The Fish and Songbird Art Contests®, Clean Drain Dry Initiative™, and Prairie City USA®. For more information, visit wildlifeforever.org.

Thank you to Ann McCarthy, the original creator of the Critters series, for her dedication to wildlife conservation and to environmental education. Ann dedicates her work to her daughters, Megan and Katharine Anderson.

Front cover photos by **Eric Isselee/shutterstock.com:** prairie dog, **JacobLoyacano/shutterstock.com:** burrowing owl, **Martha Marks/shutterstock.com:** ornate box turtle; Back cover photo by **WilliamLWatson/Shutterstock.com:** Rocky Mountain bighorn sheep

Edited by Brett Ortler and Jenna Barron
Cover and book design by Jonathan Norberg
Proofreader: Emily Beaumont

10 9 8 7 6 5 4 3 2 1

Critters of Colorado

The first *Critters* books were produced by Wildlife Forever. AdventureKEEN is grateful for its continued partnership and advocacy on behalf of the natural world.

Published by Adventure Publications
An imprint of AdventureKEEN
310 Garfield Street South, Cambridge, Minnesota 55008
(800) 678-7006
www.adventurepublications.net
Cataloging-in-Publication data is available from the Library of Congress
ISBN 978-1-64755-431-6 (pbk.); 978-1-64755-432-3 (ebook)

Acknowledgments

I want to thank everyone who believed in and supported me over the years—a host of friends, family, and teachers. I want to especially thank my mom and my siblings Van, Bre, and TJ.

Dedication

I dedicate this book to my brother Van:
May you continue to enjoy the birds and wildlife in heaven.

This book is for all the kids who have a passion for nature and the outdoors, especially ones who identify as Black, Brown, Indigenous, and People of Color. May this be an encouragement to never give up. And if you have a dream and passion for something, pursue it relentlessly. I also hope to set an example that you can be successful as your full, authentic self!

Lastly, I dedicate this book to all those with ADHD and dyslexia, as well as all other members of the neurodivergent community. While our quirks make things more challenging, our goals are not impossible to reach; sometimes it takes a little more time and help, but we, too, can succeed!

Contents

Reptiles and Amphibians

Introduction

My passion for nature started when I was young. I was always amazed by the sunlit fiery glow of the red-tailed hawks as they soared overhead when I went fishing with my family. The red-tailed hawk was my spark bird—the bird that captures your attention and gets you into birding. Through my many encounters with red-tailed hawks, and other species like garter snakes and coyotes, I found a passion for nature and the environment. Stumbling across conservationists like Steve Irwin, Jeff Corwin, and Jack Hanna introduced me to the field of Wildlife Biology as a career and gave birth to a dream that I was able to accomplish and live out: serving as a Fish and Wildlife Biologist for governmental agencies, as well as in the private sector.

My childhood dream was driven by a desire to learn more about the different types of ecosystems and the animals that call our wild places home. Books and field guides like this one whet my thirst for knowledge. Even before I could fully understand the words on the pages, I was drawn to books and flashcards that had animals on them. I could soon identify every animal I was shown and tell a fact about it. I hope that this edition of *Critters of Colorado* can be the fuel that sustains your passion for not only learning about wildlife, but also for caring for the environment and making sure that all are welcome in the outdoors. For others, may this book be the spark that ignites a flame for wildlife preservation and environmental stewardship. I hope that this book inspires children from lower socioeconomic and minority backgrounds to pursue their dreams to the fullest and be unapologetically themselves.

By profession, I'm a Fish and Wildlife Biologist, and I'm a nature enthusiast through and through. My love for nature includes making sure that everyone has an equal opportunity to enjoy the outdoors in their own way. So, as you use this book, I encourage you to be intentional in inviting others to appreciate nature with you. Enjoy your discoveries and stay curious!

–Alex Troutman

Colorado: The Centennial State

Colorado is known for its beautiful landscapes, where you can both hike in the desert and ski in the mountains. Before it was a state, though, it was the stomping ground for the now-extinct mammoths and mastodons (both large, hairy, elephant-like creatures). Many of their fossils are found in Colorado, along with evidence of humans hunting them! Indigenous tribes such as the Utes, Cheyenne, Apache, Shoshone, and the Arapaho have long lived in Colorado. In fact, the Ancestral Pueblo people built the structures now found in modern-day Mesa Verde National Park. European history in Colorado begins with the arrival of the Spanish conquistadors in the 1500s. Colorado's territory was overseen by the French, Spanish, and later Mexico, before becoming a US State in 1876.

Colorado is a land-locked state, meaning that it does not touch the ocean. In fact, at the southwest point of the rectangular state, there is a place where you can be in Colorado, Utah, Arizona, and New Mexico all at once! One of the most famous natural landmarks is the Rocky Mountains, which take up most of western Colorado and are home to animals like bighorn sheep and golden eagles. While the Rocky Mountains extend far beyond Colorado, the state is home to the highest peak in the Rockies: Mount Elbert (14,440 feet). The eastern part of the state has the Great Plains, a huge grassland perfect for roaming bison.

These environments are home to many animals, including 130 species of mammals, around 473 species of birds, and more than 65 species of reptiles and amphibians, not to mention fish, countless insects and spiders, plants, and more. This is your guide to the animals, birds, reptiles, and amphibians that call Colorado home.

Some of Colorado's most iconic plants, animals, and other natural resources are now officially recognized as state symbols. Get to know them below and see if you can spot them all! You'll probably encounter the state nickname and motto, so I've included them here too.

State Bird: lark bunting

State Cactus: claret cup cactus

 State Tree: Colorado blue spruce

 State Flower: Rocky Mountain columbine

State Fish: greenback cutthroat trout

State Amphibian: western tiger salamander

 State Reptile: western painted turtle

 State Animal: Rocky Mountain bighorn sheep

State Nickname: The Centennial State

State Butterfly: Colorado hairstreak

State Motto: *Nil sine Numine* ("Nothing without the divine will")

How to Use This Guide

This book is your introduction to some of the wonderful critters found in Colorado; it includes 21 mammals, 30 birds, and 13 reptiles and amphibians. It includes some animals you probably already know, such as deer and bald eagles, but others you may not know about, such as horned lizards or ptarmigans. I've selected the species in this book because they are widespread (northern raccoon, page 34), abundant (black-capped chickadee, page 60), or well-known, but best observed from a safe distance (common snapping turtle, page 126).

The book is organized by types of animals: mammals, birds, and reptiles and amphibians. Within each section, the animals are in alphabetical order. If you'd like to look for a critter quickly, turn to the checklist (page 140), which you can also use to keep track of how many animals you've seen! For each species, you'll see a photo of the animal, along with neat facts and information on the animal's habitat, diet, its predators, how it raises its young, and more.

Safety Note

Nature can be unpredictable, so don't go outdoors alone, and always tell an adult when you're going outside. All wild animals should be treated with respect. If you see one—big or small—don't get close to it or attempt to touch or feed it. Instead, keep your distance and enjoy spotting it. If you can, snap some pictures with a camera or make a quick drawing using a sketchbook. If the animal is getting too close, is acting strangely, or seems sick or injured, tell an adult right away, as it might have rabies, a disease that can affect mammals. The good news is there's a rabies vaccine, so it's important to visit a doctor right away if you get bit or scratched by a wild animal.

Notes About Icons

Each species page includes basic information about an animal, from what it eats to how it survives the winter. The book also includes information that's neat to know; in the mammals section, each page includes a simple track illustration of the animal, with approximate track size included. And along the bottom, there is an example track pattern for the mammal, with the exception for those that primarily glide or fly (flying squirrels and bats).

On the left-hand page for each mammal, a rough-size illustration is included that shows how big the animal is when compared to a basketball.

Also on the left-hand page, there are icons that tell you when each animal is most active: nocturnal (at night), diurnal (during the day), or crepuscular (at dawn/dusk), so you know when to look. If an animal has a "zzz" icon, it hibernates during the winter. Some animals hibernate every winter, and their internal processes (breathing and heartbeat) slow down almost entirely. Other animals only partially hibernate, but this still helps them save energy and survive through the coldest part of the year.

nocturnal
(active at night)

diurnal
(active during day)

crepuscular
(most active at
dawn and dusk)

hibernates/deep sleeper
(dormant during winter)

ground nest

cup nest

platform nest

cavity nest

migrates

On the left-hand side of each bird page, the nest for the species is shown, along with information on whether or not the bird migrates; on the right-hand side, there's information on where it goes.

Did you know?

Badgers are solitary animals, but they will sometimes hunt with coyotes in a team. A coyote will chase prey into the badger's den, and the badger will chase or dig out the prey that coyotes like. The badger's den has one entrance with a pile of dirt next to it. When a badger is threatened, it will back into its burrow and show its teeth.

Size Comparison   Most Active   Track Size   Hibernates

         2¾"

American Badger

Taxidea taxus

Size: 2–3 feet long; weighs 8–25 pounds

Habitat: Savannas, grasslands, and meadows

Range: Can be found throughout most of Colorado and westward through the Great Plains to the West Coast and southward to Mexico

Food: Carnivores; they eat pocket gophers, moles, ground squirrels, and other rodents. They will also eat dead animals (or carrion), fish, reptiles, and a few types of birds, especially ground-nesting birds.

Den: Badgers are fossorial (a digging animal that spends a lot of time underground); they build many dens or burrows throughout their range. Most dens are used to store food, but badgers also use dens to sleep in and raise their young. Dens can be over 10 feet deep and 4 feet wide.

Young: Cubs are born, with eyes closed, usually in April or May in litters of 2–3. Extensive care is provided by the mom for up to 3 months. After another 2–3 months, the young will gain their independence.

Predators: Bears, bobcats, cougars, coyotes, gray wolves, golden eagles, and humans

Tracks: The front tracks are 2¾ inches long and 2 inches wide.

The American badger is a short, bulky mammal with grayish to dirty-red fur. Badgers have a distinctive face with a series of cream-and-white stripes offset by a black background.

Did you know?

Beavers are rodents! Yes, these flat-tailed mammals are rodents, like rats and squirrels. In fact, they are the largest native rodents in North America. Just like other rodents, beavers have large incisors, which they use to chew through trees to build dams and dens. Beavers are the original wetland engineers. By damming rivers and streams, beavers create ponds and wetlands.

Size Comparison   Most Active   Track Size

6"

14

American Beaver

Castor canadensis

Size: Body is 25–30 inches long; tail is 9–13 inches long; weighs 30–70 pounds

Habitat: Wooded wetland areas near ponds, streams, and lakes

Range: Beavers can be found throughout Colorado, as well as much of the rest of the US.

Food: Leaves, twigs, and stems; they also feed on fruits and aquatic plant roots. Throughout the year they gather and store tree cuttings, which they eat in winter.

Den: A beaver's home is called a lodge. It consists of a pile of branches that is splattered with mud and vegetation. Lodges are constructed on the banks of lakes and streams and have exits and entrances that are underwater.

Young: Young beavers (kits) are born in late April through May and June in litters of 3–4. After two years they are considered mature and will be forced out of the den.

Predators: Bobcats, cougars, bears, wolves, and coyotes. Human trappers are major predators too.

Tracks: A beaver's front foot looks a lot like your hand; it has five fingers. The hind (back) foot is long, with five separate toes that have webbing or extra skin between them.

Beavers range from dark brown to reddish brown. They have a stocky body with hind legs that are longer than the front legs. The beaver's body is covered in dense fur, but its tail is naked and has special blood vessels that help it cool or warm its body.

Did you know?

Bison are the largest hoofed animals in North America. The bison's thick coat offers protection from the natural elements. In the winter, the coat acts as insulation for the bison by trapping body heat under the fur and preventing snow on its back from melting. Bison can jump 6 feet off the ground and can run around 35 miles per hour!

Size Comparison   Most Active   Track Size

5"

16

Bison
Bison bison

Size: 6 feet tall; 6½–11 feet long; weighs 1,000–2,500 pounds

Habitat: Savannas, wetlands, grasslands, river valleys, shrubland prairies, and farmlands

Range: At one time, bison roamed throughout a large portion of the US, Canada, and areas of Mexico. Today, wild populations are now limited, with many living in national parks and refuges. Other populations are considered livestock. In Colorado, they can be found in managed herds scattered across the state.

Food: Bison are herbivores that eat grasses and plants.

Den: No den. Young are born able to walk and travel.

Young: Females give birth to one 55–70-pound calf 9½ months after breeding. Calves can stand shortly after birth. The young bison will wean (no longer drink mother's milk) around 6½–7 months. Females are reproductively mature at around 2–3 years old, while males are mature at around 6 years old.

Predators: Few predators can take down a healthy adult, but mountain lions, bears, and wolves can prey on young, old, or injured bison.

Tracks: Bison tracks are 4½–5 inches long and have a similar shape to cows' hooves.

Adults are dark brown with thick, coarse hair. They have shaggy hair and horns on their head. They have a large, muscular hump on their back.

Did you know?

Female bears weigh between 90 and 300 pounds and are smaller than the average adult human male in the US. But don't let their small size fool you; with a bite force around 800 pounds per square inch (PSI) and swiping force of over 400 pounds, these bears are not to be taken lightly.

Size Comparison   Most Active   Track Size   Hibernates

6–7"

Black Bear

Ursus americanus

Size: 5–6 feet long (nose to tail); weighs 90–600 pounds

Habitat: Forests, lowland areas, and swamps

Range: Black bears can be found in many parts of North America, from Alaska down through Canada and into Mexico. In Colorado, they are found throughout the western half of the state.

Food: Berries, fish, seeded crops, small mammals, wild grapes, tree shoots, ants, bees, beavers, and even deer fawns

Den: Denning usually starts in December, with bears emerging in late March or April. Dens can be either dug (out of a hillside, for example) or constructed with materials such as leaves, grass, and moss.

Young: Two cubs are usually born at one time (a litter), often in January. Cubs are born without fur and blind, with pink skin. They weigh 8–16 ounces.

Predators: Humans and other bears. Sometimes, other carnivores, such as mountain lions, wolves, coyotes, or even bobcats, will prey on black bears. Cubs are especially vulnerable.

Tracks: Front print is usually 4–6 inches long and 3½–5 inches wide, with the hind foot being 6–7 inches long and 3½–5 inches wide. The feet have five toes.

Black bears are usually black in color, but they can be many different variations of black and brown. Some even have grayish, reddish, or blonde fur.

Did you know?

Black-footed ferrets are the only ferret species native to North America. A group of ferrets is called a business. Ferrets sleep over 20 hours a day. Their body is the same width from their neck down to their hips.

Size Comparison   Most Active   Track Size

1¾"

Black-footed Ferret

Mustela nigripes

Size: 16–24 inches long; weighs 2–3 pounds

Habitat: Grasslands, shrublands, and prairies

Range: At one time, they were found in 12 states across the US and portions of Mexico and Canada. Now, they are only found in isolated reintroduced populations in a few states, including Colorado.

Food: Carnivores that mainly eat prairie dogs, they also eat rodents and other small animals.

Den: Underground burrow; most of the time they use abandoned prairie dog burrows that are further excavated (dug out).

Young: 1–6 kits are born after a 35–45-day pregnancy. Kits will stay in the burrow for about 6 weeks (42 days) before coming out. Kits will separate by the fall of their birth year and become reproductively mature at 1 year old.

Predators: Owls, hawks, badgers, coyotes, and bobcats

Tracks: Tracks are around 1¾ inches long and 1 inch wide.

Black-footed ferrets have long, slender bodies and claws that are yellowish brown to black. They have a buffy-light-brown underside, with blackish feet and a dark mask around their widely spaced eyes. Their ears and tails sport a black tracing. They have a round face with a short muzzle and legs.

Did you know?
Even though they are called prairie dogs, they are not in the canine or dog family; they are actually rodents belonging to the squirrel family. The black-tailed is the most common of the prairie dog species. Prairie dogs use a variety of vocalizations to communicate. They will even "bark" to alert others to danger.

Size Comparison   Most Active   Track Size

         1–2"

Black-tailed Prairie Dog

Cynomys ludovicianus

Size: 14–17 inches long; weighs 2–3 pounds

Habitat: Grassy plains and prairies

Range: They are found in the Great Plains east of the Rocky Mountains and into Mexico. In Colorado, they can be found in the eastern portion of the state.

Food: Grasses, seeds, plants, and sometimes insects

Den: They live in multi-burrow colonies called "towns." Burrows can be 3–6 feet wide, sometimes as deep as 15 feet underground, and have several chambers. The nest chamber is usually lined with grass.

Young: One litter of 3–5 pups is born after 30–35 days of pregnancy. Pups are born hairless and blind. They open their eyes around 5 weeks and will start exploring outside the burrow around the same time. Both parents care for young and, once they are aboveground, any female producing milk will nurse them. They will leave the coterie (group of prairie dogs) at 1 year old.

Predators: Black-footed ferrets are their main predators; snakes, eagles, coyotes, hawks, falcons, and badgers.

Tracks: The front foot is 1–1½ inches long and hind foot is 1–2 inches long. Both sets are ⅞–1⅜ inches wide with claw marks at the end of each toe.

Prairie dogs come in various shades of brown and tan. They have small, thick bodies; rounded ears; a short tail; sharp teeth; and strong claws for digging. Their tail is black at the tip, hence their name.

Did you know?

At one time, coyotes were only found in the central and western parts of the US, but now, with the help of humans (eliminating predators and clearing forests), they can be found throughout most of the country.

Size Comparison   Most Active   Track Size

2"

Coyote
Canis latrans

Size: 3–4 feet long; weighs 21–50 pounds

Habitat: Urban and suburban areas, woodlands, grasslands, and farm fields

Range: Coyotes can be found in all the counties of Colorado. They are also found throughout the US and Mexico, the northern parts of Central America, and in southern Canada.

Food: A variety of prey, including rodents, birds, deer, and sometimes livestock

Den: Coyotes will dig their own dens but will often use old fox or badger dens or hollow logs.

Young: 5–7 pups, independent around 8–10 months

Predators: Bears and wolves; humans trap and kill for pelts and to "protect" livestock.

Tracks: Four toes and a carpal pad (the single pad below the toe pads) can be seen on all four feet.

Coyotes have brown, reddish-brown, or gray back fur with a lighter gray-to-white belly. They have a longer muzzle than other wild canines. They are active mostly during the night (nocturnal) but also during the twilight and dawn hours (crepuscular).

Did you know?

At over 280,000 animals, Colorado's elk population is the largest in the world. Elk are known to be the loudest of all cervids (deer family). Males produce a low-pitched bellow or roar, called a bugle. Bugling is a technique that involves both roaring and whistling at the same time. Elk use their bugle or bugling to attract mates or announce territories during the fall mating season. Their bugles can be heard over long distances.

Size Comparison   Most Active   Track Size

4½"

Elk
Cervus elaphus canadensis

Size: 5–8 feet tall; weighs 377–1,095 pounds

Habitat: Open woodlands, mountain areas, shrublands, coniferous swamps, and hardwood forests

Range: Found throughout Colorado. They are found in the western US with isolated populations in the eastern US. They are also found in southern Canada.

Food: Elk are herbivores that eat grasses; flowers; and leaves from trees like cedar, red maple, and basswood.

Den: No den; will lay in grass to rest. Mother elk will hide young calves in tall grasses.

Young: Calves are born after 240–265 days. At birth, calves weigh around 30 pounds and have spots through the first summer. Separation from mother's milk happens around the 60-day mark, but calves will continue to get care and protection from mom for around a year. They reach full maturity around 16 months, but males will usually wait to mate until they are older.

Predators: Mountain lions and bears. Calves may fall victim to bobcats and coyotes.

Tracks: Front tracks of an adult are about 4¾ inches long and wide. Hind foot tracks are 4½ inches long and 3½ inches wide. Two toes are on both feet.

Elk come in different shades of browns and tans. In the summer and spring they are lighter brown to tan, while in the winter they are a deep dark brown; during both seasons, they have a cream or off-white rump. They sport a darker tone on the head, neck, belly, and legs.

27

Did you know?

Moose belong to the deer family, and they are the largest members of the deer family in the world! They can rotate their ears 180 degrees. Moose can swim over 5 miles per hour for over 8 miles, and they can also run over 35 miles per hour. Moose will dive beneath the water of ponds and lakes to reach the plants at the bottom.

Size Comparison   Most Active   Track Size

4"

Moose

Alces alces

Size: 7–10 feet long; 5–6½ feet from the shoulder to the ground; weighs 750–1,200 pounds or more

Habitat: Forested areas, marshes, wetlands, and swamps

Range: They can be found as far north as Alaska and the northern parts of the eastern US, as far west as Washington state, and as far south as the central parts of Colorado.

Food: Leaves, bark, twigs, roots, and aquatic plants

Den: Like other deer, moose dig out beds amid the forest floor.

Young: 1–2 young (calves) that are 25–35 pounds at birth; moose are considered adults at around 2 years old.

Predators: Bears, mountain lions, and humans

Tracks: Hoofprints are large and heart-shaped, measuring 4 inches long.

Moose are a deep brown with a hump on the shoulder and a dewlap (a flap of skin, which is also known as a "bell") hanging down from the throat area. Males are larger than females, and they have large, flat antlers that can be over 4 feet wide and weigh over 30 pounds.

Did you know?

Mountain lions are the second largest cat in the western part of the world. The largest is the jaguar. Mountain lions do not roar like other big cats, but rather they scream! They also make other sounds similar to pet cats, like hissing and purring. Mountain lions can jump as high as 18 feet off the ground into a tree.

Size Comparison   Most Active   Track Size

Mountain Lion

Puma concolor

Size: 6–8 feet long; weighs 100–154 pounds

Habitat: Grasslands, deserts, wetlands, shrublands, forests, swamps, and upland forests

Range: They can be seen from northern Canada to Argentina. In Colorado, they are found in foothills and canyons.

Food: Deer, wild boars, raccoons, birds, rabbits, mice, and occasionally livestock

Den: Will den in caves, rock piles and crevices, and thickets. Dens are usually lined with plants.

Young: 1–6 kittens are born with spots almost 100 days after mating. Weaning takes place around day 4, and the young kits will stay with their mom another year or two. Spots fade at around 6 months. Males reach reproductive maturity at around 3 years old and females around 2½ years, though they usually do not reproduce until they have a permanent home territory.

Predators: No natural predators, but they will sometimes get in territory disputes with other large carnivores.

Tracks: Front tracks are 3¼ inches long and wide. The back or hind tracks are 3 inches long and wide.

Mountain lions' fur is golden tan to dusky brown on the back; their underside is a pale buff color with a white throat and chest area. They have a pink nose, black ear tips, and a smoky gray-black muzzle. The tip of their tail is black like their ears, and their eyes are brown. Their tail is long and makes up a third of their body length. Kittens have spots until they are 4–5 months old, and they have smoky-blue eyes.

Did you know?

A single porcupine can have over 30,000 quills that it can use to protect itself from predators. Porcupine quills are hollow and can be over 2 inches long. Porcupines are herbivores (plant eaters), and they have a special bacteria in their digestive system to help them break down the plant material.

Size Comparison   Most Active   Track Size

3⅜"

North American Porcupine

Erethizon dorsatum

Size: 2–3 feet long; weighs 10–25 pounds

Habitat: Forested areas, grasslands, and deserts

Range: They are found throughout Colorado; they are also found throughout Canada and various areas across the northern and western US.

Food: Skunk cabbage, clovers, twigs, leaves, and tree bark

Den: They den in hollow logs and tree cavities.

Young: One young (porcupette) is born between May and July; they weigh a pound at birth and have 1-inch quills.

Predators: Lynx, bobcats, coyotes, owls, and fishers

Tracks: The front foot is shorter than the hind foot; the hind foot has five toes, while the front only has four toes.

The North American porcupine is mostly nocturnal; its fur is black to gray and shades of brown with obvious quills. When threatened, it will turn around and strike an attacker with its tail quills, which are 4 inches long and are like needles. With that many quills, porcupines sometimes accidentally poke themselves. To protect itself (from itself), the porcupine has a special substance on its quills that acts like an antibiotic (or medicine). This prevents it from getting infected after an accidental poke. Like other mammals, porcupines need salt and will chew on, or lick, objects with the mineral to fulfill that craving. Sometimes this leads to porcupines chewing on human-made structures.

Did you know?

The raccoon is great at catching fish and other aquatic animals, such as mussels and crayfish. They are also excellent swimmers, but they apparently avoid swimming because the water makes their fur heavy. Raccoons can turn their feet 180 degrees; this helps them when climbing, especially when going headfirst down trees.

Size Comparison	Most Active	Track Size	Hibernates
		3"	

Northern Raccoon

Procyon lotor

Size: 24–40 inches long; weighs 15–28 pounds

Habitat: Woody areas, grasslands, suburban and urban areas, wetlands, and marshes

Range: They are found throughout Colorado and the US; they are also found in Mexico and southern Canada.

Food: Eggs, insects, garbage, garden plants, berries, nuts, fish, carrion, small mammals, and aquatic invertebrates like crayfish and mussels

Den: Raccoon dens are built in hollow trees, abandoned burrows, caves, and human-made structures.

Young: 2–6 young (kits) are born around March through July. They are born weighing 2 ounces, are around 4 inches long, and are blind with lightly colored fur.

Predators: Coyotes, foxes, bobcats, humans, and even large birds of prey

Tracks: Their front tracks resemble human handprints. The back tracks sort of look like human footprints.

The northern raccoon has dense fur with variations of brown, black, and white streaks. It has black, mask-like markings on its face and a black-and-gray/brownish ringed tail. During the fall, it will grow a thick layer of fat to stay warm in the winter.

Did you know?

Otters are good swimmers and can close their nostrils while diving. This allows them to dive for as long as 8 minutes and to depths of over 50 feet. Otter fur is the thickest of all mammal fur. River otters have an incredible 67,000 hairs for every square centimeter!

Size Comparison   Most Active   Track Size

Northern River Otter

Lontra canadensis

Size: 29–48 inches long; weighs 10–33 pounds

Habitat: Lakes, marshes, rivers, and large streams; suburban areas

Range: Otters can be found throughout most of western Colorado, with scattered populations in the eastern portion of the state; they are found across much of the US, except parts of the Southwest and portions of the central US.

Food: Fish, frogs, snakes, crabs, crayfish, mussels, birds, eggs, turtles, and small mammals. They sometimes eat aquatic vegetation too.

Den: They den in burrows along the river, usually under rocks, riverbanks, hollow trees, and vegetation.

Young: 2–4 young (pups) are born between November and May. Pups are born with their eyes closed. They will leave the area at around 6 months old and reach full maturity at around 2 or 3 years.

Predators: Coyotes, bobcats, bears, and dogs

Tracks: Their feet have nonretractable claws and are webbed.

Northern river otters have thick, dark-brown fur and a long, slender body. Their fur is made up of two types: a short undercoat and a coarse top coat that repels water. They have webbed feet and a layer of fat that helps keep them warm in cold water.

Did you know?

Pikas are the smallest member of the rabbit family. Pikas are also called "whistling hares" because they give out loud warning calls in the presence of danger; in fact, many times you will hear a pika before you see it.

Size Comparison   Most Active   Track Size

Pika

Ochotona princeps

Size: 6½–8½ inches long; weighs 4–6½ ounces

Habitat: Mountains above the tree line, rock faces, cliffs, alpine terrain, slopes of mountain meadows, and hillsides

Range: The pika lives in southwest Canada and the western US. In Colorado, they can be found at high elevations in the Rocky Mountains, generally above 8,000 feet above sea level.

Food: Pikas are herbivores that eat grasses, weeds, and wildflowers. They will sometimes eat their own waste (poop) that is rich in protein and energy.

Den: Dens are formed in rock piles and are no larger than 3 feet.

Young: After 30 days of pregnancy, 2 litters of kits (ranging from 2–6 young) are each year. The young depend on their mother at birth. Young are weaned around a month after birth and can breed the following year.

Predators: Prairie falcons, red foxes, golden eagles, coyotes, American martens, red-tailed hawks, bobcats, and long-tailed weasels

Tracks: Front feet are ¾ inches long and ⅗ inches wide with five toes. Hind feet are 1–1¼ inches long and 2½–3½ inches wide with four toes.

Pikas are small mammals with an oval-shaped, stout body. They have big ears and short legs. Pikas have thick fir that is brown to tannish with an overlaying of black on its back.

Did you know?

The pronghorn is the fastest land animal in North America. It can reach speeds of 60 miles per hour and jump over 20 feet in distance. The pronghorn is only found in North America. Though it looks similar to an antelope, it is not related. They are more closely related to giraffes!

Size Comparison Most Active Track Size

2¾"

Pronghorn

Antilocapra americana

Size: 4½ feet long; 3½ feet to shoulder; weighs 90–150 pounds

Habitat: Grasslands, shrublands, mixed-grass prairies, brushlands, and deserts

Range: The pronghorn can be found throughout much of the western United States, down into Mexico, and northward into southern Canada. In Colorado, they can be found throughout the state, with higher numbers in the eastern plains.

Food: They are herbivores that eat grasses and sagebrush.

Den: No den; will bed in grass and use tall grass to hide young (fawns)

Young: Usually give birth to 1–2 fawns. They are able to stand within a few hours. The fawns will join the herd when they are about a week old and begin grazing when they are 3 weeks old. Fawns stay with their mother for about a year until they become independent.

Predators: Mountain lions, wolves, coyotes, bears, and eagles

Track: Front tracks are about 3¼ inches long, while the hind tracks are about 2¾ inches long.

Pronghorns are reddish tan to brown in color. They are the smallest hoofed mammals (ungulates) in Colorado. They have a white rump, belly, chest, and cheeks. The inside of their legs is also white. Males have a black mask that extends down the face from their eyes to their nose. Males have large horns that curve inward. Females have smaller horns that are usually straight; they do not have black markings on their face.

       41

Did you know?

Ringtails are also called civet cats, ringtail cats, and miner's cats, although they are not related to cats. They are related to raccoons! Their ankles can rotate 180 degrees, which allows them to go headfirst down a cliff or tree.

Size Comparison   Most Active   Track Size

3"

Ringtail
Bassariscus astutus

Size: 24 inches long (half is tail); weighs 1½–2 pounds

Habitat: Canyons, rocky outcrops, deserts, woodlands, montane forests (forests in mountains), and shrublands

Range: They are found in the southwestern US to Texas and in northern Mexico. In Colorado, they can be found in southern and central parts of the state.

Food: They are omnivores that eat fruit, insects, birds, flowers, small mammals, carrion (dead animals), seeds, amphibians, grains, bird eggs, reptiles, and nuts.

Den: Dens are usually in hollow trees, rock crevices, or boulder piles. They will also den in human structures. Dens are usually lined with grasses, moss, or leaves.

Young: Young are born blind and naked. Their eyes do not open until around day 30 or so when they start to eat solid food. They are weaned from milk around 2½ months. At around 10 months, they will reach reproductive maturity.

Predators: Bobcats, coyotes, and great horned owls

Tracks: Front feet are 1–1¾ inches long and 1¼–1½ inches wide. Hind feet are 1–1½ inches long and ¾–1¼ inches wide. Tracks have five toes.

Ringtails have a catlike body that is yellowish gray to black on their back and buffy gray on their belly. They have large ears, a pointed muzzle, and long whiskers. Their face has a black-to-brown-patterned mask with white-to-buffy eye rings. They have a long, buffy-colored tail that is separated by seven black rings.

Did you know?

The largest wild sheep in North America is the Rocky Mountain bighorn sheep. Their horns can be over 3 feet long and as thick as 1 foot and can weigh over 20 pounds. Bighorn sheep are agile, able to run over 30 miles per hour and jump over 19 feet from one ledge to another.

Size Comparison   Most Active   Track Size

2½—3½"

Rocky Mountain Bighorn Sheep

Ovis canadensis canadensis

Size: 59–71 inches long; weighs 116¾–270 pounds or more

Habitat: Alpine meadows; grassy mountain slopes; and foothill country close to rugged, rocky cliffs and bluffs

Range: Found in the Rocky Mountains of North America from southern Canada to Colorado. In Colorado, they can be found in mountainous areas throughout the state.

Food: Grasses, clovers, sedges, and flowers

Den: No den

Young: One lamb is born around 150–180 days after breeding. Young are precocial, meaning they are able to walk and stand a few minutes to hours after birth. By months 4–6, lambs are weaned. During the first year of life, they learn their home territory. Males will leave their mom at 2–4 years old to join a male group, and females will usually stay their mom for their whole life.

Predators: Wolves, coyotes, golden eagles, bears, Canada lynx, and mountain lions

Tracks: Front and hind tracks are 2½–3½ inches long and 1¾–2½ inches wide.

Both male and female bighorn sheep are light to dark brown; they sometimes have a grayish hue. Their muzzle, backs of legs, and rump are white. The males (rams) have large, circular horns that frame their face. Females (ewes, pronounced like "yous") have shorter horns that are not as circular. Young (lambs) are grayish with a blackish-brown tail.

Did you know?

The largest population of swift foxes in North America is in Colorado. It is one of North America's smallest native canids (member of the dog family), and it is slightly bigger than the kit fox. The swift fox gets its name due to its ability to run up to 25 miles per hour.

Size Comparison   Most Active   Track Size

1½"

Swift Fox

Vulpes velox

Size: 23–34 inches long; weighs 4–7 pounds

Habitat: Hillsides, prairies, deserts, ranchlands, and plains

Range: They can be found in western Canada and down through the Great Plains of the United States. In Colorado, they can be found in the eastern part of the state.

Food: Small mammals, fruit, amphibians, grains, berries, fish eggs, carrion (dead animals), reptiles, birds, insects, grasses, seeds, and nuts

Den: Dens are made in open prairies in sandy soils; they often construct their own but will also use dens made by other animals. Dens have multiple entrances and are at least 1 meter (about 3 feet) underground.

Young: 3–6 pups are usually born after a 50–60-day pregnancy. They will emerge from the den about a month later. Pups are born with eyes closed; they will open around 10–15 days after birth. Both parents care for the young, and pups are weaned (stop drinking milk) around 6–7 weeks. Males will reach reproductive maturity in their first winter and females usually in their second winter.

Predators: Coyotes, raptors, and badgers

Tracks: Both tracks are about 1½ inches long with 4 toes.

Swift foxes' fur is tannish orange with salt-and-pepper color on their back, sides, and legs. Their chest, belly, and the inside of their legs are white. In the summer, they have shorter fur that is a deeper red in color.

Did you know?

The opossum is the only marsupial native to the US. Marsupials are a special group of animals that are most well-known for their pouches, which they use to carry their young. When frightened, young opossums will play dead (called playing possum) and adults will show their teeth and hiss or run away.

Size Comparison   Most Active   Track Size

2½"

Virginia Opossum

Didelphis virginiana

Size: 22–45 inches long; weighs 4–8 pounds

Habitat: Forests, woodlands, meadows, and suburban areas

Range: They are found throughout Colorado; they are found throughout the eastern US, Canada, and also in Mexico and Costa Rica.

Food: Eggs, small mammals, garbage, insects, worms, birds, fruit, and occasionally small reptiles and amphibians

Den: They den in hollow trees, abandoned animal burrows, and buildings.

Young: A litter of 6–20 young (joeys) are born blind and without fur; their limbs are not fully formed. Young will climb from the birthing area into the mother's pouch and stay until 8 weeks old; they then alternate between the mother's pouch and her back for 4 weeks. At 12 weeks they are independent.

Predators: Hawks, owls, pet cats and dogs, coyotes, and bobcats

Tracks: The front feet are 2 inches long and around 1½ inches wide and resemble a child's hands; the hind feet are 2½ inches long and around 2¼ inches wide; they have fingers in front with a fifth finger that acts as a thumb.

The Virginia opossum has long gray-and-black fur; the face is white, and the tail is pink to gray and furless. Opossums have long claws.

Did you know?
When they first emerge, a deer's antlers are covered in a special skin called velvet. Deer can run up to 40 miles per hour and can jump over 8 feet vertically (high) and over 15 feet horizontally (across).

Size Comparison   Most Active   Track Size

3"

White-tailed Deer

Odocoileus virginianus

Size: 4–6 feet long; 3–4 feet tall at front shoulder; weighs 114–308 pounds

Habitat: Forest edges, brushy fields, wooded farmlands, prairies, and swamps

Range: They are found throughout Colorado and throughout the US, except for much of the Southwest; they are also found in southern Canada and into South America.

Food: Fruits, grass, tree shrubs, nuts, and bark

Den: Deer do not den but will bed down in tall grasses and shrubby areas.

Young: Deer usually give birth to twins (fawns) that are 3–6 pounds in late May to June. The fawns are born with spots; this coloration helps them hide in vegetation. Young become independent at 1–2 years.

Predators: Wolves, coyotes, bears, bobcats, and humans

Tracks: Both front and hind feet have two teardrop- or comma-shaped toes.

Crepuscular (active at dawn and dusk), white-tailed deer have big brown eyes with eye rings and a long snout with a black, glossy nose. The males have antlers, which fall off each year. All deer have a white tail that they flash upward when alarmed. Deer molt or change fur color twice a year. They sport rusty-brown fur in the summer; in early fall, they transition to winter coats that are grayish brown in color.

Did you know?

The marmot is the largest ground squirrel found in Colorado. In winter, marmots spend about 80% of their time hibernating in burrows that may be as deep as 16 feet or more.

Size Comparison   Most Active   Track Size

2—2½"

Yellow-bellied Marmot

Marmota flaviventris

Size: 16½–28 inches long; weighs 3½–11 pounds

Habitat: Alpine meadows, fields, pastures, and rocky areas

Range: Marmots are widespread in western North America. They can be found throughout the central and western parts of Colorado.

Food: They are herbivores that eat flower stalks, grasses, flowers, and seeds.

Den: Dens consist of an underground burrow with a complex internal structure and multiple nesting areas. Nesting chambers are usually away from activity and toward the end of the burrow under a large rock and lined with grasses.

Young: 30 days after breeding, a litter of 3–8 pups is born. Pups will leave the nest at about 3 weeks old and are fully weaned around week 5. Males are driven from the nest by older adult males just after hibernation. Females will stay in the group. They reach maturity around 2 years old but will not mate until year 3.

Predators: Coyotes, hawks, weasels, owls, bobcats, golden eagles, and badgers

Tracks: Four toes on the front feet and five on the hind feet. Front feet are 1½–2½ inches long and 1–1½ inches wide. Hind feet are 2–2½ inches long and wide.

Yellow-bellied marmots are thick-bodied rodents of the squirrel family. They are brown with white spots on their chin and a yellow belly and feet. They have a dark head with small ears and a short muzzle.

Did you know?

The American goldfinch helps restore habitats by spreading seeds. The goldfinch gets its color from a pigment called a carotenoid (say it, cuh-rot-en-oid) in the seeds it eats. It can even feed upside down by using its feet to bring seeds to its mouth.

Nest Type

Most Active

Migrates

American Goldfinch

Spinus tristis

Size: 4½–5 inches long; wingspan of 9 inches; weighs about half an ounce

Habitat: Grasslands, meadows, suburban areas, and wetlands

Range: Found throughout most of Colorado during the non-breeding season; they can be found in far northern parts of the state as year-round residents. They are found all over the US.

Food: Seeds of plants and trees; sometimes feeds on insects; loves thistle seeds at birdfeeders

Nesting: Goldfinches build nests in late June.

Nest: Cup-shaped nests are built a couple of feet above-ground out of roots and plant fibers.

Eggs: 2–7 eggs with a bluish-white tint

Young: Young (chicks) hatch around 15 days after being laid; they hatch without feathers and weigh only a gram. Chicks learn to fly after around 11–15 days. Young become mature at around 11 months old.

Predators: Garter snakes, blue jays, American kestrels, and cats

Migration: Populations in the northern portion of the state are year-round residents, while the southern populations migrate north to breed and return to overwinter in Colorado.

During the summer, American goldfinch males are brightly colored with golden-yellow feathers and an orange beak. They have black wings with white wing bars. The crown (top) of the head is black. In winter, they molt, and the males look more like the females. Females are always greenish yellow with hints of yellow around the head.

Did you know?
The bald eagle is an endangered species success story! The bald eagle was once endangered due to a pesticide called DDT that weakened eggshells and caused them to crack early. Through the banning of DDT and other conservation efforts, the bald eagle population recovered, and it was removed from the Endangered Species List in July of 2007.

Nest Type   Most Active   Migrates

Bald Eagle

Haliaeetus leucocephalus

Size: 3½ feet long; wingspan of 6½–8 feet; weighs 8–14 pounds

Habitat: Forests and tree stands (small forests) near river edges, lakes, seashores, and wetlands

Range: They are a resident bird throughout Colorado; they are found throughout much of the US.

Food: Fish, waterfowl (ducks), rabbits, squirrels, muskrats, and deer carcasses; will steal food from other eagles or osprey

Nesting: Eagles have lifelong partners that begin nesting in fall, laying eggs between November–February.

Nest: They build a large nest out of sticks, high up in trees; the nest can be over 5 feet wide and over 6 feet tall, often shaped like an upside-down cone.

Eggs: 1–3 white eggs

Young: Young (chicks) will hatch at around 35 days; young will leave the nest around 12 weeks. It takes up to 5 years for eagles to get that iconic look!

Predators: Few; collisions with cars sometimes occur.

Migration: Many migrate to Colorado during winter, with over 200 breeding pairs being year-round residents.

Adult bald eagles have a dark-brown body, a white head and tail, and a golden-yellow beak. Juvenile eagles are mostly brown at first, but their color pattern changes over their first few years. A bald eagle can use its wings as oars to propel itself across bodies of water.

Did you know?
Kingfishers inspired human technology! Bullet trains around the world are designed after the kingfisher's beak, which allows it to dive into water without a splash. This design was used in bullet trains to allow them to enter into tunnels without making a large booming sound. This process of modeling human technology after animal features is called biomimicry.

Nest Type

Most Active

Migrates

Belted Kingfisher
Megaceryle alcyon

Size: 11–13¾ inches long; wingspan is 19–24 inches; weighs 5–6 ounces

Habitat: Forests and grassland areas near rivers, ponds, lakes

Range: Year-round resident of Colorado, as well as most of the US; in other areas of the US and Canada.

Food: Carnivores, they eat mostly fish and other aquatic animals, such as crayfish and frogs, and occasionally other birds, mammals, and berries.

Nesting: Nests are in the form of upward-sloped burrows that are dug in soft banks on or near water. (The upward slopes prevent flooding.)

Nest: Females and males select the nest site together; males do most of the digging.

Eggs: 5–8 white, smooth, glossy eggs are laid per clutch (group of eggs).

Young: Chicks are born featherless with pink skin, closed eyes, and a dark bill. They receive care from both parents. Chicks leave the nest after about 28 days.

Predators: Snakes, hawks, and mammals

Migration: Mostly a resident bird; in some areas, will migrate south during nonbreeding season

The belted kingfisher is bluish gray on top; the bottom half is white with a blue/gray belt or band. The wings have white spots on them. Unlike most other birds, the kingfisher female has a different pattern than the male. Females have a second reddish-brown or rusty-orange band on their belly.

Did you know?

Black-capped chickadees have a unique strategy for surviving winter. The area of the brain that aids in memory (the hippocampus) temporarily gets bigger in preparation for winter. This allows them to remember where they hid or cached seeds.

Nest Type   Most Active

Black-capped Chickadee

Poecile atricapillus

Size: 5½–7½ inches long; wingspan of 8 inches; weighs about half an ounce

Habitat: Forests, woodland edges, and suburban and urban areas

Range: They are year-round residents of Colorado and can be found in the northern United States.

Food: Caterpillars, insects, seeds, spiders, and berries

Nesting: April to August

Nest: Chickadees utilize old woodpecker holes or make their own cup-shaped nests in tree cavities that have been weakened by rot.

Eggs: 4–6 eggs that are white with brown spots

Young: Eggs hatch 12–13 days after they are laid; chicks leave the nest around 15 days after hatching; chickadee parents continue feeding the young for another 5–6 weeks.

Predators: Hawks, owls, shrikes, raccoons, house cats left outside, and other mammals

Migration: They do not migrate.

A black-capped chickadee has a gray body with a black cap, or top of head, and a black throat and beak; they have white cheeks and light bellies.

Did you know?

The brown-capped rosy-finch is one of three species of rosy-finches found in North America. Brown-capped rosy-finches will sometimes use old or abandoned mines as nesting areas because they provide shelter from bad weather.

Nest Type   Most Active

Brown-capped Rosy-finch

Leucosticte australis

Size: 5½–6¼ inches long; wingspan of 13 inches; weighs ¾–1¼ ounces

Habitat: Mountainous areas, alpine tundra and meadows, forests, cliffs, and other rocky environments

Range: Restricted to the Rocky Mountains in Colorado, New Mexico, and southern Wyoming. They are year-round residents throughout their range.

Food: Seeds, insects, and spiders

Nesting: March–August

Nest: Females build nests in caves, on cliffs, and even in mines. Nests are made of grasses, roots, and other plant material. They are often lined with fur and feathers.

Eggs: 3–6 white eggs are laid per year.

Young: Young hatch helpless and with down feathers. They receive food from both parents. Chicks will leave the nest around 18 days after hatching.

Predators: Hawks, owls, and squirrels

Migration: They move to higher elevation to breed and to lower elevation in winter.

The brown-capped rosy-finch is a small bird with a short tail. The breeding male has a chocolate-brown back and upper chest. Their lower chest, rump, and outer wings are rosy-red. They have a dark-brown-to-slate-gray cap or upper head area. The bill and legs are also dark. The females are similar in color to nonbreeding males but are less vibrant and have a yellow bill. Juveniles are brown with black-and-brown-streaked wings and light hues of pinks on their wings and belly.

Did you know?

Burrowing owls are fossorial, meaning that they live and/or spend most of their day underground. They will sometimes mimic rattlesnakes when threatened, by hiding in a burrow and making rattling and hissing sounds. They like to decorate their mounds with scat, or poop, from mammals. It is believed that the scat helps to attract insects to eat and to hide the scent of the owl's young.

Nest Type   Most Active

Burrowing Owl

Athene cunicularia

Size: 7½–11 inches long; wingspan of 20–22 inches; weighs 5–6 ounces

Habitat: Savanna forest, urban and suburban areas, farmlands, shrublands, prairies, deserts, and mountains

Range: They can be found from southern Canada down into Mexico and as far east as Minnesota and Texas. They can be found throughout Colorado during the breeding season.

Food: Carnivores; mostly insects and rodents, but also amphibians, reptiles, birds, and rarely seeds and fruit

Nesting: March–April

Nest: Nests in burrows usually made by other animals. The male will line the nesting burrow with plants, feathers, scat, and sometimes trash.

Eggs: 4–12 white eggs often tinted the color of the dirt

Young: Owlets hatch 3–4 weeks after laying, covered with down that is gray or white. Within 4 weeks, they are able to fly short distances and explore areas outside of the burrow. They will receive care for another 1–3 months until they can hunt.

Predators: Snakes, pet cats and dogs, foxes, skunks, hawks, falcons, weasels, and other owl species; humans play a heavy role in displacement and loss of habitat.

Migration: Year-round residents who do not migrate

Burrowing owls are small, brown owls adorned by white spots of various sizes on their back. They have a white or creamy belly with brown bars. They have large yellow eyes with thick white eyebrows and throat.

Did you know?
The canvasback is the largest diving duck in North America.
They are able to dive up to 30 feet, but they usually only dive
around 7 feet. Females have an interesting nesting strategy:
they will lay eggs in another canvasback's nest.

Nest Type   Most Active   Migrates

Canvasback Duck

Aythya valisineria

Size: 19–22 inches long; wingspan of 31–35 inches; weighs 30½–56½ ounces

Habitat: Lakes, estuaries, wetlands, deep-water marshes, lagoons, bays, and ponds

Range: They can be found throughout Colorado as winter residents. They are widespread across most of the US and central and western Canada.

Food: They are omnivores that eat seeds, mussels, plants, insects, and fish.

Nesting: Mating pairs form during spring migration. Females select the nest spot.

Nest: Bulky platform nests are usually built over water in shallow wetlands among cattails and other plants like reeds. The nest is also sometimes built on land.

Eggs: 5–11 greenish eggs per clutch, 2½ inches long and 1¾ inches wide

Young: After 24–28 days, chicks hatch covered in down and are precocial, meaning they can leave the nest within a few hours after hatching. Chicks will fledge at around 10 weeks and reach reproductive maturity at 1 year.

Predators: Bald eagles, mink, snapping turtles, raccoons, hawks, owls, black-crowned night herons, and other large predators

Migration: Migrates north to breeding grounds in the spring

Breeding males have a chestnut-brown head with a black chest area and rump. Their body is whitish with intricate markings that look like canvas. Females are pale brown. Males have red eyes, while females have black eyes. Both have a long bill.

Did you know?

Cinnamon teals fly in large, synchronized or coordinated groups that complete impressive flights with abrupt turns and dives. Cinnamon teals will hide their nest in tall vegetation and use tunnels to get to their nest. Cinnamons are closely related to blue-winged teals and will sometimes breed with them.

Nest Type   Most Active   Migrates

Cinnamon Teal

Spatula cyanoptera

Size: 15–17 inches long; wingspan of 21¼–22½ inches; weighs 11¾–14 ounces

Habitat: Wetlands, estuaries, mangrove swamps, and reservoirs

Range: They can be found throughout much of Colorado as breeding residents; they are widespread in the western half of the US and southern Canada, as well as Mexico.

Food: They are omnivores that eat snails, seeds, zooplankton (microscopic organisms), aquatic plants, dragonflies, and other insects.

Nesting: Females select the nest site.

Nest: Nests are shallow scraped depressions lined with grasses, weeds, and other plant material. Down feathers are often placed in the nest as eggs are laid.

Eggs: 9–12 whitish to cream-colored eggs are laid. Eggs are about 2 inches long and 1½ inches wide.

Young: Young hatch 21–25 days after eggs are laid. They are covered in yellowish down feathers at hatching. Young are precocial (able to walk and swim); within moments of hatching, they are led to water. Young will fledge at 7 weeks and are reproductively mature at 1 year.

Predators: Pet cats and dogs, crows, American mink, coyotes, gulls, magpies, raccoons, and other ducks

Migration: Migrate south to wintering grounds after breeding

Cinnamon teals are small ducks. Females, immatures, and non-breeding males are brown to buffy brown. Breeding males have a burnt-red-to-rusty-colored body, dark-colored bill, and red eyes. Both adult males and females have a light-blue patch of feathers that are only visible when the wing is open.

Did you know?

The double-crested cormorant does not have oil glands like other aquatic birds; this is why you will see it on a rock or a post with its wings spread: it's drying itself off. The cormorant's bill curves at the end, perfect for grasping fish and other prey.

Nest Type

Most Active

Migrates

Double-crested Cormorant

Nannopterum auritum

Size: 26–35 inches long; wingspan of 45–48½ inches; weighs 2½–3 pounds

Habitat: Freshwater lakes, rivers, swamps, coastal waters

Range: They can be found across North America. In Colorado, they can be found statewide.

Food: They are carnivores that eat fish, insects, snails, and crayfish.

Nesting: April–August; male chooses the nest site before finding a female. Nest in groups with other water birds

Nest: Veteran parents may repair an old nest. Otherwise, they build a new nest on the ground or in a tree. Nests are made of sticks and lined with grass. Nests can be as wide as 3 feet and over 1½ feet tall.

Eggs: On average, 4 light-bluish-white eggs are laid at a time.

Young: Young chicks (shaglets) usually hatch in 25–28 days; they can swim immediately after hatching.

Predators: Eggs are vulnerable to raccoons, gulls, jays, foxes, and coyotes. Adults and chicks are preyed on by coyotes, foxes, raccoons, eagles, and great horned owls.

Migration: They migrate south in winter.

Adults have black feathers and topaz-colored eyes, with an orange bill, throat, and face area; they have black feet that are webbed like a duck's. The tail is short. During breeding season, adults may have a "double crest" of black feathers or sometimes white, depending on the location. This is where they get their name. Young are all brown or black.

Did you know?

The dusky grouse was once called the blue grouse; in 2006, it was determined that the blue grouse was actually two different species: the dusky grouse and the sooty grouse. The dusky grouse is the second-largest grouse found in North America. Instead of running or flying, dusky grouse will use their plumage (feathers) as camouflage and sit still in order to hide from predators.

Nest Type   Most Active

Dusky Grouse

Dendragapus obscurus

Size: 17–22½ inches long; wingspan of 24–27 inches; weighs 2–3 pounds

Habitat: Forests, grasslands, and shrubby habitats

Range: They can be found across western North America from Canada down into New Mexico and Arizona. In Colorado, they can be found in the center of the state, with a range that widens both eastward and westward toward the southern part of the state.

Food: They are omnivores that eat insects, leaves, flowers, berries, and tree needles of conifer species.

Nesting: Prior to nesting, males perform a special dance. They strut with their tail fanned out and neck feathers spread to show off patches of pink-to-red skin.

Nest: Nests are shallow scraped depressions on the ground. Nests are made by the female and are lined with feathers, leaves, needles, moss, and bark.

Eggs: 5–10 white eggs with brown markings.

Young: After 25–28 days, chicks hatch from the eggs with downy feathers. They leave the nest within 1–2 days and become independent at around 2–3 months old.

Predators: Owls, hawks, black bears, eagles, red foxes, coyotes, mountain lions, and bobcats

Migration: Year-round residents who will migrate to lower elevations during the breeding season

Dusky grouse are large, ground-dwelling birds. The males are bluish or slate gray. Females are duller brown to gray. Males have an orange-to-yellow spot over each eye. Males will reveal a deep red-pink patch of skin on their neck during mating displays.

Did you know?

This is the largest of the North American hawks. Ferruginous and rough-legged hawks (plus golden eagles) are the only American hawks to have feathered legs all the way down to their toes. Their common name "ferruginous" means "rust-colored" or "reddish-brown." In winter, groups of five or more hawks sometimes gather in prairie dog towns to hunt the prairie dogs as they emerge from underground.

Nest Type   Most Active   Migrates

Ferruginous Hawk

Buteo regalis

Size: 22–27¼ inches long; wingspan of 52½–56 inches; weighs 34½–73¼ ounces

Habitat: Open spaces, prairies, cliffs, outcrops, deserts, grasslands, sagebrush, scrubland, and woodland edges

Range: They can be found in the western US, southern Canada, and Mexico. In Colorado, they are year-round residents throughout, breeding residents in the northwest, and winter residents in the central parts.

Food: Carnivores, they eat small, ground-dwelling mammals; amphibians; birds; insects; and reptiles.

Nesting: Male and female choose a nest site in a tree, cliff, building, outcrop, boulder, shrub, or haystack.

Nest: Bulky nests made of sticks, bones, plastic, and metals

Eggs: 2–4 creamed-colored eggs with brown splotches are laid. Female does the most incubating, while the male brings her food.

Young: Chicks hatch after 32–33 days with eyes closed, covered in down, and helpless. Chicks are fed by the female with food hunted by the male. Chicks will take their first flight at around day 50. They will reach reproductive maturity at around 2 years.

Predators: Eagles, prairie falcons, great horned owls, coyotes, and foxes can all prey on eggs and young.

Migration: Year-round with some short-distance migrants

Ferruginous hawks have broad wings and feathered legs. Their wings and back are a rusty-to-brown color, and they have a grayish-to-white-and-rusty tail. They have a white head with dark-brown-to-black streaking.

Did you know?

Golden eagles are the largest bird of prey that actively hunts in North America! They are North America's second-largest bird of prey after the California condor, which is a scavenger. Golden eagles also have the widest range of all eagles. They can be found across North America, Africa, Europe, and Asia. Several countries have named the golden eagle as their national bird, including Mexico, Albania, Kazakhstan, and Austria.

Nest Type   Most Active   Migrates

Golden Eagle

Aquila chrysaetos

Size: 26–33 inches long; wingspan of 6–8 feet; weighs 7½–9 pounds

Habitat: Shrublands, forests, mountains, cliffs, canyons, grasslands, rocky areas, and woodlands

Range: Widespread across North America; in Colorado, they are year-round and breeding residents.

Food: Birds, goats, sheep, coyotes, pronghorns, badgers, reptiles, deer, fish, bobcats, and small mammals

Nesting: January–May

Nest: Nests on cliffs, trees, and buildings. Nests are made of sticks and other plant materials; they will sometimes include animal bones and human objects.

Eggs: 2–3 cream-to-light-pink eggs are laid

Young: Eaglets hatch about 40–45 days after eggs are laid. They learn to fly at around 10 weeks. They will reproduce at around 4–7 years.

Predators: Wolverines and grizzly bears are the major predators of chicks. Humans are often the cause of death due to habitat loss and hunting practices.

Migration: Mostly year-round residents in Colorado; in the northeastern area of the state, they will migrate north.

Golden eagles are covered in dark-brown feathers. They have a golden neck and sides of their face, which is where they get their name. They have broad wings that stretch over 7 feet across. The tail is faded brown to dark brown. They have deep-brown eyes, a black-tipped bill, and black claws. Their feet are yellow, and their legs are covered with feathers. Immature eagles have patches of white-to-buffy-colored feathers.

77

Did you know?

The catbird can make over 100 different types of sounds, including one song that can last well over 5 minutes. Catbirds are intelligent; they are one of the few species of songbirds that can recognize and remove brown-headed cowbird eggs when they are abandoned in their nests. Brown-headed cowbirds will lay their eggs in the nests of other birds and make them raise their young.

Nest Type   Most Active   Migrates

Gray Catbird

Dumetella carolinensis

Size: 8¼–9½ inches long; wingspan of 8¾–11¾ inches; weighs ¾–2 ounces

Habitat: Shrubs, urban (city) areas, vine tangles, and thickets

Range: Gray catbirds can be found in most parts of North America as breeding residents, and year-round residents along the eastern coast. In Colorado, they can be found throughout the state as breeding residents.

Food: Ants, flies, beetles, moths, grasshoppers, caterpillars, and spiders. They also eat various fruits and berries.

Nesting: Starts in April and goes to early August. The female builds the nest, and the male will supply materials sometimes. The male guards the nest while the female incubates the eggs. Both care for chicks.

Nest: Females build cup nests with twigs, mud, bark, and straw, lined with grass, fur, and pine needles.

Eggs: Clutch size is 3–6 eggs that are teal or turquoise green.

Young: Chicks are born 12–14 days after laying. At hatching, they are naked except for spots of dark down feathers and have their eyes closed. Chicks leave the nest at around 10 days. They receive care for another 12 days or so. They can reproduce at 1 year.

Predators: Pet cats and dogs, foxes, skunks, coyotes, and raptors

Migration: In fall, they migrate to more southern areas, including Texas. During breeding season, they migrate north.

Catbirds are medium-size songbirds. They are slate gray with a black tail. They have a small cinnamon- to rust-colored patch at the base of their tail. Their head is gray with a black cap.

Did you know?

The great blue heron is the largest and most common heron species. A heron's eye color changes as it ages. The eyes start out gray but transition to yellow over time. Great blue herons swallow their prey whole.

Nest Type   Most Active   Migrates

Great Blue Heron

Ardea herodias

Size: 3–4½ feet long; wingspan of 6–7 feet; weighs 5–7 pounds

Habitat: Lakes, ponds, rivers, marshes, lagoons, wetlands

Range: They can be found throughout Colorado, as well as the entirety of the United States and down into Mexico.

Food: Fish, rats, crabs, shrimp, grasshoppers, crayfish, other birds, small mammals, snakes, and lizards

Nesting: May–August

Nest: 2–3 feet across and saucer shaped; often grouped in large rookeries (colonies) in tall trees along the water's edge. Nests are built out of sticks and are often located in dead trees more than 100 feet above the ground; nests are used year after year.

Eggs: 3–7 pale bluish eggs

Young: Chicks will hatch after 28 days of incubation; young will stay in the nest for around 10 weeks. They reach reproductive maturity at just under 2 years.

Predators: Eagles, crows, gulls, raccoons, bears, and hawks

Migration: Populations in western areas of the state will fly south to southern states, the Caribbean, and Central America to overwinter, and fly north to breed. Most of Colorado has year-round residents.

The great blue heron is a large wading bird with blue and gray upper body feathers; the belly area is white. They have long yellow legs that they use to stalk prey in the water. Great blue herons are famous for stalking prey at the water's edge; their specially adapted feet keep them from sinking into the mud!

Did you know?

A great horned owl can exert a crushing force of over 300 pounds with its talons. Despite its name, the great horned owl doesn't have horns at all. Instead, the obvious tufts on its head are made of feathers. Scientists aren't sure exactly how the tufts function, but they may help them stay hidden.

Nest Type

Most Active

Great Horned Owl

Bubo virginianus

Size: Up to 23 inches long; wingspan of 45 inches; weighs 3 pounds

Habitat: Woods; swamps; desert edges; as well as heavily populated areas such as cities, suburbs, and parks

Range: They are found throughout Colorado and the continent of North America.

Food: They eat a variety of foods, but mostly mammals. Sometimes they eat other birds as well.

Nesting: They have lifelong partnerships, with nesting season starting in early winter; egg-laying starts in mid-January–February.

Nest: Nests are found 20–50 feet off the ground. They tend to reuse nests from other raptors or hollowed-out trees.

Eggs: The female lays 2–4 whitish eggs. Eggs are incubated for around 30 days.

Young: Young can fly at around 9 weeks old. The parents care for and feed young for several months.

Predators: Young owls are preyed upon by foxes, coyotes, bears, and opossums. As adults, they are rarely attacked by other birds of prey, such as golden eagles and goshawks.

Migration: Great horned owls are not regular migrators, but some individuals will travel south during the winter.

They are bulky birds with large ear tufts, a rusty brown-to-grayish face with a black border, and large bright eyes. The body color tends to be brown; the wing pattern is checkered with an intermingled dark brown. The chest and belly areas are light brown and have white bars.

Did you know?

Downy woodpeckers are the smallest woodpecker species in North America. Hairy woodpeckers can hear insects traveling under the tree bark. Downy woodpeckers have a built-in mask, or special feathers, near their nostrils that helps them to avoid breathing in wood chips while pecking.

Nest Type   Most Active

Hairy/Downy Woodpecker

Leuconotopicus villosus/Dryobates pubescens

Size: Hairy: 7–10 inches long; wingspan of 13–16 inches; weighs 3 ounces. Downy: 5½–7 inches long; wingspan of 10–12 inches; weighs less than an ounce

Habitat: Forested areas, parks, woodlands, and orchards

Range: Throughout Colorado and across the United States

Food: Hairy: beetles, ants, caterpillars, fruits, and seeds. Downy: beetles, ants, galls, wasps, seeds, and berries

Nesting: Hairy: March to June. Downy: January to March

Nest: In both woodpecker species, pairs will work together to create a cavity. Both parents also help to incubate eggs.

Eggs: Hairy: 3–7 white eggs. Downy: 3–8 white eggs

Young: Hairy woodpeckers' eggs will hatch 2 weeks after being laid and then fledge (develop enough feathers to fly) after another month. Downy woodpeckers' eggs will hatch after about 12 days and fledge 18–21 days after hatching. Both species hatch blind and featherless.

Predators: American kestrels, snakes, sharp-shinned hawks, pet cats, rats, squirrels, and Cooper's hawks

Migration: Woodpeckers are mostly year-round residents, but some in the north may travel south during the winter.

Hairy woodpeckers and downy woodpeckers look strikingly similar with their color pattern. One way to distinguish them is to look at the size of the body and bill. The downy woodpecker is smaller than the hairy woodpecker and has a shorter bill. If you look at the tail feathers of the two species, you will also see that the hairy woodpecker does not have black spots, while the downy's tail does.

Did you know?
The lark bunting is the state bird of Colorado! The male lark bunting is the only species of the sparrow family that changes its entire plumage during the winter and breeding season. One name for a group of buntings is a "mural."

Nest Type Most Active Migrates

Lark Bunting

Calamospiza melanocorys

Size: 5½–7 inches long; wingspan of 9¾–11 inches; weighs 1¼–1½ ounces

Habitat: Roadsides, open grasslands, mixed-grass prairies, hayfields, and farm fields

Range: They can be found from southern Canada to the Great Plains and into northern Mexico. In Colorado, some are migrants, whereas others are breeding residents.

Food: They are omnivores that feed on grasshoppers, ants, grasses, moths, cactus fruit, seeds, grains, weeds, and beetles.

Nesting: Early June to early August; males set up and defend territories, and females select the nest site. Both birds will build the nest.

Nest: Cup-shaped nests are made on the ground with grass, weeds, and roots, and lined with animal hair and other plants.

Eggs: 4–5 light-blue eggs are laid per brood.

Young: Hatchlings are born with down feathers and eyes closed. Chicks leave the nest 7–9 days after they hatch.

Predators: Pet cats, snakes, hawks, owls, rats, and ground squirrels

Migration: Migrates in the fall and winter

Breeding males are a brilliant, deep tuxedo-black with an area of white on part of their wings called coverts. Immatures and females are dusky brown with white in the wings that is visible when the wings are open or in flight. During the winter, the males' plumage will change to resemble the females and immature males in color.

Did you know?
The Lewis's woodpecker's wing beats are so much slower than other woodpeckers that it is often confused for a crow. The Lewis's woodpecker spends most of its time grabbing insects off the bark and sides of trees instead of digging into trees for insects like other woodpeckers.

Nest Type   Most Active   Migrates

Lewis's Woodpecker

Melanerpes lewis

Size: 10¼–11 inches long; wingspan of 19¼–20½ inches; weighs 3–5 ounces

Habitat: Open pine forests, oak woodlands, burned forests, orchards, and farming areas

Range: Can be found in southwestern Canada and the western half of the US. In Colorado, they are year-round residents in the central and western part of the state; some also breed in northwestern Colorado.

Food: They are omnivores that eat insects, nuts, and fruits.

Nesting: Late April–July

Nest: They nest in a cavity or hole in a dead or decaying tree. They usually will use existing cavities or holes, even enlarging them sometimes. Nests are lined with wood chips at the bottom.

Eggs: 5–9 white eggs are laid per brood.

Young: Chicks hatch after 12–16 days of incubation, featherless and with eyes closed. They receive food from both adults and will leave the nest after 28–34 days.

Predators: Pet cats, bobcats, snakes, foxes, squirrels, and hawks

Migration: Year-round resident in most of Colorado; breeding adults will migrate north to breeding areas.

Lewis's woodpeckers are medium-size birds with an iridescent green-black back. They have a pink-to-reddish belly and a dark-red face and gray collar on the neck that extends down to their chest. Juveniles are similar to adults but have brownish heads and chests.

Did you know?

When viewed straight-on, the yellow portion on the mallard's bill resembles a cartoon dog's head. Most domesticated ducks share the mallard as their ancestor. mallard feathers are waterproof; they use oil from the preen gland beneath their feathers to help aid in repelling water. Mallards are the most common duck in the United States and Colorado.

Nest Type	Most Active	Migrates

Mallard

Anas platyrhynchos

Size: 24 inches long; wingspan of 36 inches; weighs 2½–3 pounds

Habitat: Lakes, ponds, rivers, and marshes

Range: They are found throughout Colorado; the population stretches across the United States and Canada into Mexico and as far up as central Alaska.

Food: Insects, worms, snails, aquatic vegetation, sedge seeds, and grasses

Nesting: April–August

Nest: The nest is constructed on the ground, usually near a body of water.

Eggs: 9–13 eggs

Young: Eggs hatch 26–28 days after being laid. The ducklings are fully feathered and have the ability to swim at the time of hatching. Ducklings are cared for until they're 2–3 months old and reach reproductive maturity at 1 year old.

Predators: Humans, crows, mink, coyotes, raccoons, and snapping turtles

Migration: After breeding season, many birds migrate south; some may stay if food and shelter is available.

Male mallards are gray with an iridescent green head with a tinge of purple spotting, a white line along the collar, rusty-brown chest, yellow bill, and orange legs and feet. Females are dull brown with a yellow bill, a bluish area near the tail, and orange feet.

Did you know?

Like other bluebirds, mountain bluebirds do not have blue pigment in their feathers; the "blue" color we see is from the feathers absorbing all wavelength of color except for blue. The blue is reflected, and that is what is visible to us! Mountain bluebirds hover over and pounce on their prey, unlike other bluebird species.

Nest Type

Most Active

Migrates

Mountain Bluebird

Sialia currucoides

Size: 6¼–8 inches long; wingspan of 11–14¼ inches; weighs a little over 1 ounce

Habitat: Mountain meadows, hillsides, woodlands, open areas, prairies, and pastures

Range: They can be found in Alaska into Canada, the western US, and Mexico. In Colorado, they are found year-round in the central part of the state. Overwintering birds are found in eastern Colorado, and others nest in far northwestern Colorado.

Food: Insects, insects, spiders, berries, and seeds

Nesting: March–August; males usually arrive to breeding site first and scout for a nesting cavity. Females select site while the males defend the nesting territory.

Nest: The female builds the nest by herself in an existing cavity with dry grass, stems, and other plant material; sometimes animal hair and feathers are used.

Eggs: 4–8 pale-blue-to-white eggs (usually 2 broods per year)

Young: Chicks hatch after 13–17 days of incubation. They receive care from both parents. Chicks will leave the nest at around 17–23 days after they hatch.

Predators: Hawks, falcons, owls, weasels, mice, squirrels, raccoons, snakes, and chipmunks

Migration: Some migrate; others are found year-round

Mountain bluebirds are stocky birds with a rounded head and small, black, pointed bill. They have black legs and feet. The males are dark sky-to-royal blue with a white underside. The female has dull, blue-gray wings and a gray underside, back, and head.

Did you know?
A mourning dove eats around 12% or more of its body weight each day. Mourning doves will store seeds and grain in their crop (pouch on their neck). Some people mistake the mourning dove call for an owl call.

Nest Type

Most Active

Migrates

Mourning Dove

Zenaida macroura

Size: 8–14 inches long; wingspan of 17–19 inches; weighs 3½–6 ounces

Habitat: Woodlands, parks, grasslands, scrub areas, farm fields, and suburban and urban areas

Range: In Colorado, it can be found throughout the state; it is abundant throughout southern Canada and the continental United States.

Food: Fruit, insects, and seeds; young feed on crop milk

Nesting: Courtship begins in April.

Nest: Males will show females several potential nesting sites. The female will choose the site, the male will bring nest-building materials to the female, and she will then construct the nest.

Eggs: 2 white eggs, incubated by both parents

Young: Within 2 weeks, hatchlings will depart the nest, but they receive care for another week or so.

Predators: Cats, falcons, hawks, raccoons, and humans

Migration: Year-round residents that don't migrate

Mourning doves are gray and brown. They have a brown chest and pointed tail that has a white tip on it. Their beak is grayish-black, the eyes are black, and on their head just below the eyes they have a black spot. They can be recognized by their spooky "hoo, hoo, hoo" call or the whistling of their wings when they take off.

Did you know?

The osprey is nicknamed the "fish hawk" because it is the only hawk in North America that mainly eats live fish. An osprey will rotate its catch to put it in line with its body, pointing headfirst, which allows for less resistance in flight as the air travels over the fish.

Nest Type   Most Active   Migrates

Osprey
Pandion haliaetus

Size: 21–23 inches long; wingspan of 59–71 inches; weighs 3–4½ pounds

Habitat: Near lakes, ponds, rivers, swamps, and reservoirs

Range: Seen in migration and during the summer, it can be found in all of Colorado and throughout the US.

Food: Feeds mostly on fish; they sometimes eat mammals, birds, and reptiles if there are few fish.

Nesting: For ospreys that migrate, egg-laying happens in April and May. The female will take on most of the incubation of the eggs, as well as the jobs of keeping the offspring warm and providing protection.

Nest: Platform nests are constructed out of twigs and sticks. Nests are constructed on trees, snags, or human-made objects like cellular towers and telephone poles.

Eggs: The mother lays 1–3 cream-colored eggs; they have splotches of various shades of brown and pinkish red on them.

Young: Chicks hatch after around 36 days and have brown-and-white down feathers. Ospreys fledge around 50–55 days after hatching and will receive care from parents for another 2 months or so.

Predators: Owls, eagles, foxes, skunks, raccoons, and snakes

Migration: Ospreys migrate south to wintering areas in the fall.

Ospreys are raptors, and they have a brown upper body and white lower body. The wings are brown on the outside and white on the underside, with brown spotting and streaks toward the edge. The head is white with a brown band that goes through the eye area, highlighting the yellow eyes.

Did you know?

The peregrine falcon is the fastest diving bird in the world. A peregrine falcon can reach speeds over 200 miles per hour (mph) when diving. To aid in diving and maneuvering in the air, like most other birds, peregrine falcons have a third eyelid called a nictitating membrane that helps to keep out debris and wind.

Nest Type

Most Active

Migrates

Peregrine Falcon

Falco peregrinus

Size: 14–19½ inches long; wingspan of 39–43 inches; weighs 1–3½ pounds

Habitat: Hardwood forests, coastal areas and marshes, urban areas, orchards, backyards, and fields

Range: They are found throughout the lower western part of the state as year-round residents, and as breeding and nonbreeding residents in much of the rest of the state. They can be found throughout North America.

Food: Carnivores, they feed on pigeons, songbirds, aquatic birds, rodents, and sometimes bats

Nesting: February–March. Pairs mate for life and reuse nests. The female chooses a nest site and will scrape a shallow hole in loose soil or sand. Nests are usually on cliff edges or tall buildings. Sometimes they even use abandoned nests of other large birds.

Nest: Shallow ground scrapes about 8–9 inches wide and 2 inches deep with no extra nesting materials added

Eggs: 3–5 off-white-to-brown eggs speckled brown or purple

Young: 30 days after eggs are laid, chicks (or eyas) will hatch with eyes closed and covered in off-white down.

Predators: Great horned owls, golden eagles, and humans

Migration: Falcons in eastern Colorado migrate.

The female is slightly larger than the male. Peregrine falcons have gray wings with black-to-gray, bar-like marks and deep-black wing tips. The breast and belly areas are covered with black-to-brown horizontal streaks or bars. They have a black head and black marks below the eyes. The neck is white. The beak, legs, eye rings, and feet are yellow.

Did you know?

The sandhill crane is the most abundant crane species in the world. They are not afraid to defend themselves when threatened. They will use their feet and bill to ward off predators, often stabbing attackers with their bill. Sometimes sandhill cranes will travel 500 miles in one day to find food.

Nest Type Most Active Migrates

Sandhill Crane

Grus canadensis

Size: 3½–4 feet long; wingspan of 6–7 feet; weighs 7½–10 pounds

Habitat: Grasslands, savannas, and farm fields

Range: Breeding resident in western North America. They can be found during migration in many states. They are mostly migrating residents that can be found throughout most of Colorado, and breeding residents can be found in the northwestern corner of the state.

Food: Berries, insects, snails, amphibians, and small mammals as well as food crops like corn

Nesting: Nonmigratory populations will lay eggs from December–August, while populations that migrate will nest between April and May.

Nest: Both adults build the cup-shaped nest using vegetation from nearby areas.

Eggs: Up to 3 pale brownish-yellow eggs with brown spots

Young: Chicks are born with the ability to see and walk. Chicks become independent at around 9 months and will start breeding between 2 and 7 years.

Predators: Coyotes, raccoons, ravens, great horned owls, and humans

Migration: Cranes arrive in late March to early May and migrate south from September to December.

The sandhill crane is a large bird with gray to brownish feathers with a white face and ruby-red crown. They are commonly seen in large groups in fields.

Did you know?
Short-eared owls make their nests on the ground. Males will use wing claps to attract mates during a courtship display.

Nest Type   Most Active   Migrates

Short-eared owl

Asio flammeus

Size: 13½–17 inches long; wingspan of 33½–40½ inches; weighs 7¼–16¾ ounces

Habitat: Grasslands, rock quarries, savannas, marshes, dunes, gravel pits, thickets, and coastal grasslands

Range: Seen throughout Colorado in the winter and a year-round resident in northern Colorado, as well as much of the US.

Food: Mice, voles, shrews, moles, lemmings, rabbits, pocket gophers, bats, rats, weasels, and birds

Nesting: March–June

Nest: Ground-scraped bowl is made by female and lined with grasses and down feathers. Nests are usually built on ridges or hummocks where vegetation can hide them.

Eggs: 4–7 creamy-white eggs, 1½–1¾ inches long and 1½ inches wide

Young: Chicks are hatched 21–37 days after laying with eyes closed and downy feathers. They will fledge 12–18 days after hatching and fly within another 9–10 days.

Predators: Ravens and crows, dogs, skunks, foxes, and coyotes

Migration: Some owls migrate north to breeding areas, while others are year-round residents.

Short-eared owls have short tufts of feathers, rounded heads, and are medium-size. They have a pale-to-white face with yellow eyes that are outlined in black. They have broad wings and a short tail. Their body is brown with spots of white, and they have a pale chest with streaks of brown.

Did you know?

This is the tanager species that has the northernmost breeding territory in northwest Canada. They get their red color on their heads from a chemical in the insects they eat, while other birds get their color from chemicals in the plants they eat.

Nest Type   Most Active   Migrates

Western Tanager

Piranga ludoviciana

Size: 6¼–7½ inches long; wingspan of 11½ inches; weighs ¾–1¼ ounces

Habitat: Mixed forests, open woodlands, forest edges, wetlands, neighborhood parks, and gardens

Range: They can be found through the western half of the United States, Canada, and Mexico. In Colorado, they can be found throughout the western half of the state as a breeding resident and in the eastern half of the state during migration.

Food: Omnivores, they eat fruit but mostly insects such as ants, wasps, caterpillars, beetles, and grasshoppers.

Nesting: Males start to defend territory in late spring and summer. Nests are built mostly by females.

Nest: Shallow cup nests are made of twigs and grasses and are lined with animal hair and roots. Nests are mostly placed in the fork of a tree.

Eggs: 3–5 bluish-green or pale-blue eggs, sometimes with gray-brown spots, are laid per brood.

Young: After 13 days, young hatch covered with down feathers and eyes closed. Chicks receive care from both parents. Young will leave the nest 2 weeks after hatching.

Predators: Hawks, snakes, owls, black bears, and pet cats

Migration: Migrates northward from Mexico and central America during the breeding season and leaves in fall

Male western tanagers sport a bright-yellow body, black wings, and a reddish orange head. Females and immatures are a duller yellow-to-olive green with gray-to-faded-black wings. Both sexes have two pairs of white wing bars, plus a black back and tail.

Did you know?

White-tailed ptarmigans (the P is silent) are the smallest species of grouse found in North America. They go through a plumage change during the winter and summer months. During the winter, they are all white; in the summer, they sport a streaked-brown, speckled plumage with shades of gray mixed in. They have built-in "snowshoes," or special feathers on their feet that help them walk on top of the snow.

Nest Type   Most Active

White-tailed Ptarmigan

Lagopus leucura

Size: 11¾–12¼ inches long; wingspan of 22 inches; weighs 11½–17 ounces

Habitat: In the winter: alpine tundra, rocky areas, and melting snowfields; in the summer: areas above tree line with short plants and streams

Range: They can be found from Alaska down into Canada and several states in the West; it is a year-round resident throughout Colorado.

Food: Fruit, leaves, buds, flowers, and seeds

Nesting: In the spring, the male guards a female while she selects a nesting area.

Nest: Females build a ground nest by scraping plant material into a circle. Vegetation and some feathers are added to the circle until the female is ready to incubate.

Eggs: 2–8 light-brown eggs are laid; eggs gain brown spots as they get closer to hatching.

Young: Chicks hatch covered in down with eyes open and are able to leave the nest within hours. Young feed themselves at hatching. Within 10–12 days, they can fly and reach adult size with 12–14 weeks.

Predators: Eagles, hawks, owls, foxes, weasels, and blackbirds

Migration: They are permanent residents.

The white-tailed ptarmigan is a small grouse with black eyes that is completely white in the winter and streaked brown with shades of gray in the summer. Breeding males have red eye combs, or areas above their eyes. They sport a band of black-and-brown feathers across their chest. Their white tail stays white all year long, and that is where they get their name.

107

Did you know?

Turkeys sometimes fly at night, unlike most birds, and land in trees to roost. Turkeys have some interesting facial features; the red skin growth on a turkey's face above the beak is called a snood, while the growth under the beak is called a wattle. Wild turkeys can have more than 5,000 feathers.

Nest Type   Most Active

Wild Turkey

Meleagris gallopavo

Size: 3–4 feet long; wingspan of 5 feet; males weigh 16–25 pounds; females weigh 9–11 pounds

Habitat: Woodlands and grasslands

Range: Found throughout Colorado. They also can be found in the eastern US and have been introduced in many western areas of the country.

Food: Grain, snakes, frogs, insects, acorns, berries, and ferns

Nesting: April–September

Nest: The nest is built on the ground using leaves as bedding, in brush or near the base of trees or fallen logs.

Eggs: 10–12 tan eggs with very small reddish-brown spots

Young: Poults (young) hatch about a month after eggs are laid; they will flock with the mother for a year. When young are still unable to fly, the mom will stay on the ground with her poults to provide protection and warmth. When poults grow up, they are known as a hen if they are female, or a gobbler or tom if they are male.

Predators: Humans, foxes, raccoons, owls, eagles, skunks, and fishers

Migration: Turkeys do not migrate.

A wild turkey is a large bird that is dark brown and black with some iridescent feathers. Males will fan out their tail to attract a mate. When threatened, they will also fan out their tail and rush the predator, sometimes kicking and puncturing prey with the spurs on their feet.

Did you know?
Wood ducks will "mimic" a soccer player when a predator is near their young: they flop! Female wood ducks will fake a broken wing to lure predators away from their young. Wood duck hatchlings must jump from the nest after hatching to reach the water. They can jump 50 feet or more without hurting themselves.

Nest Type   Migrates

Wood Duck

Aix sponsa

Size: 15–20 inches long; wingspan of 30 inches; weighs about 1 pound

Habitat: Swamps, woody ponds, and marshes

Range: They are mostly nonbreeding residents throughout Colorado, but they can be found in a section of eastern Colorado as year-round residents and a small tip of northern Colorado; they are also in the eastern US, southern Mexico, the Pacific Northwest, and on the West Coast.

Food: Fruits, nuts, and aquatic vegetation, especially duckweed, sedges, and grasses

Nesting: March–August

Nest: Wood ducks use hollow trees, abandoned woodpecker cavities, and human-made nesting boxes.

Eggs: 8–15 off-white eggs are laid once a year. Sometimes females will lay eggs in another female's nest; this process is called egg dumping.

Young: Eggs hatch about a month after being laid. Chicks will leave the nest after a day and fly within 8 weeks.

Predators: Raccoons, mink, fish, hawks, snapping turtles, owls, humans, and muskrats

Migration: They are nonbreeding residents in much of Colorado but migrate to breeding areas during the fall.

Wood duck males have a brightly colored crest (tuft of feathers) of iridescent (shimmering) green, red, and purple, with a mahogany (brown) upper breast area and tan bottom. Males also have red eyes. Females are brown to gray. Wood ducks have strong claws that enable them to climb up trees into cavities.

111

Did you know?
When they are in danger or threatened, eastern collared lizards
will stand up and run on their hind legs. They can reach speeds
over 15 miles per hour to escape predators.

Most Active

Eastern Collared Lizard

Crotaphytus collaris

Size: 8–14 inches long; weighs 2 to 4½ ounces

Habitat: Rocky canyons, cliffs, shrublands, flat canyon bottoms, woodlands, areas with exposed bedrock, and gullies

Range: They can be found in northern Mexico and several western states. In Colorado, they can be found in the southern portion of the state.

Food: Small snakes, grasshoppers, moths, spiders, beetles, and other lizards

Mating: Mid-May–early June

Nest: Burrow dug beneath a large rock

Eggs: 4–10 eggs per clutch are laid within 20 days after breeding; may lay a second clutch.

Young: Hatchlings hatch 2–2½ months after being laid. They experience a rapid growth and are large enough to mate at around 1 or 2 years. Hatchlings' sex is dependent on egg temperature during incubation.

Predators: Coyotes, bobcats, lizards, birds, pet cats, snakes, foxes, and hawks

The eastern collared lizard sports a large head and long tail. Breeding males are various shades of tans with bright blues and greens and a bright-yellow head. They have irregular spots or blotches across their body. Females are brownish to green in color. Females that are carrying eggs have spots on their bodies that fade after they have laid their eggs. Both males and females have one irregular black line that sits just behind the head, with a second broader and wider line that extends across the neck and stops at the top of the front limbs. Juveniles are yellow with a collar that resembles the adults. They have a series of orange-to-yellowish blotches down their body.

Did you know?

The eastern painted turtle is the largest of the subspecies of painted turtles. It can breathe through its butt! Known technically as "cloacal breathing," this adaptation enables them to hibernate underwater. They still need to breathe, of course, but their body slows down so much that the oxygen they absorb through blood vessels in their behind is enough for them to survive.

Most Active   Hibernates

Eastern Painted Turtle

Chrysemys picta

Size: Male is 7 inches long; female is 10–12 inches long; males weigh 10–12 ounces; females weigh around 18 ounces

Habitat: Marshes, small lakes, ponds, wetlands, and swamps

Range: They are found across much of eastern Colorado and a small area in the southwestern part of the state.

Food: Fish, plants, tadpoles, dead animals, crayfish, and insects

Mating: Late spring and fall

Nest: The turtle digs a hole in soil/sand adjacent to a body of water.

Eggs: 8–9 oval eggs; eggs have a soft shell.

Young: Hatchlings emerge from the nest between August and September; young rely on the egg yolk for food for the first few days of life. In their first year, they can double their size. Females reach reproductive maturity around 11–16 years, while males reach it around 7–9 years.

Predators: Snapping turtles, raccoons, opossums, foxes, mink, skunks, cats, humans, and fish

The eastern painted turtle's skin is black with two yellow stripes that line the head. The carapace (top shell) is black, while the plastron (bottom shell) is yellow or even red sometimes. Painted turtles can be found basking in groups. In the North, turtles hibernate during the winter by burying themselves in the bottom of bodies of water or near water on the bank, sometimes even using mammal burrows. Painted turtles can live over 35 years in the wild, although most do not live to be that old.

115

Did you know?

Females can produce over 45,000 eggs, but the average is usually around 10,000. The temperature can affect the rate that Great Plains toads go through metamorphosis; if the temperature is too warm and the water that they are living in is in risk of drying out, they undergo the process faster. The males let out a long, loud trill during the breeding season to attract mates.

Most Active

Great Plains Toad

Anaxyrus cognatus

Size: 2–3½ inches long; weighs 2 ounces

Habitat: Plains, grasslands, sandhills, farm areas, and semi-desert shrublands

Range: They are found in portions of southern Canada and several states of the Midwest and southwestern United States. They are found in eastern Colorado.

Food: Worms, beetles, ants, and other insects

Mating: Breeds mainly in late spring and early summer, in pools, ponds, and reservoirs

Nest: No nest is built; females use shallow bodies of water (no more than 12 inches deep) to lay eggs in.

Eggs: Females lay around 11,000 eggs at one time. Eggs are laid in a row of long strings that are nestled in two layers of jelly. Females can lay over 20,000 eggs in one season.

Young: Tadpoles hatch 2–7 days after being laid. Tadpoles metamorphose or change into small toads in about 2 months. They reach maturity within 3–5 years.

Predators: Raccoons, water bugs, fish, hognose snakes, grackles, and skunks

Great Plains toads can be identified by their round snout, dry warty skin, and large eyes that sit on the top of their head. They have two ridges or crests above each eye that combine and make a bump on their snout called a "boss." They come in various colors of creams to tans, with blotches of darker tans, browns, and greens covering their body. They have a large parotid gland behind each eye. Their underside is light brown to cream with no spots.

Did you know?

While ornate box turtles are mainly land dwellers, they are able to float and swim decently due to fat deposits under their shells. During the winter, they bury themselves in sandy soil to avoid freezing.

Most Active

Hibernates

Ornate Box Turtle

Terrapene ornata

Size: 4½–5 inches long; weighs ½–1½ pounds

Habitat: Forests, open grasslands, pastures, shrublands, wetlands, farm fields, and marsh meadows

Range: Can be found as far north as Wisconsin, as far east as Louisiana, as far west as Arizona, and as far south as Texas into Mexico. They can be found in eastern Colorado.

Food: Omnivores, they eat earthworms, berries, beetles, grasses and other plants, and carrion (dead animals).

Mating: Late spring–early summer

Nest: Shallow, flask- shaped burrow built in loose material (dirt, soil, sandy clay)

Eggs: 2–8 eggs

Young: Hatchlings hatch 75–90 days after eggs are laid and will reach reproductive maturity at around 5 years for males and 8 years for females.

Predators: Crows, ravens, hawks, owls, raccoons, cats, foxes, and snakes

Ornate box turtles have sharp beaks, thick limbs, and a flattened dome-shaped carapace (top of shell). The carapace is brownish to black and has a starburst-like pattern on it. The skin is grayish brown with orange-to-yellow spots. They have a yellow or pale-greenish chin. Males have red-hued legs and a large inner claw. Males also have reddish eyes, while females have brown. Males are usually smaller than females.

Did you know?

Plains hognose snakes are venomous! But luckily, their venom is not harmful to us. Hognoses' fangs have a dual purpose: to inject venom into prey and to deflate frogs or toads who may puff their bodies up. The hognose uses some interesting techniques to ward off would-be predators. First, the snake will flatten its head to look like a cobra. Then, if that doesn't work, it will play dead by flipping over and letting its tongue hang out of its mouth.

Most Active   Hibernates

Plains Hognose Snake

Heterodon nasicus

Size: 15–40 inches long; weighs 60–120 grams or about 5 ounces

Habitat: Prairies, neighborhoods, pastures, canyons, floodplains, scrub brush, farm fields, deserts, and montane woodlands

Range: From southern Canada down into western Minnesota, southward to central and eastern Texas, and eastern New Mexico. In Colorado, they can be found along the eastern half of the state.

Food: Small birds, turtles, lizards, smaller snakes, mammals, eggs, ants, beetles, and grasshoppers

Nest: Females dig out nests in loose sandy soil and lay eggs; sometimes, eggs are laid in a row in a tunnel instead of clustered together.

Eggs: 2–24 oval eggs that are white or cream in color. Eggs for this species have smooth, leathery shells.

Young: Hatchlings are more brightly colored than adults. They reach maturity at around 2–3 years for females and 1–2 years for males.

Predators: Hawks, crows, and coyotes

Plains hognose snakes are small, thick-bodied snakes with an upturned or shovel-shaped snout. They come in various shades of brown and tan with 20–55 darker brown blotches that run down their back. Along their sides, they have two alternating rows of spots that travel the length of their body. They have several dark lines that run the length of their face from corner to corner; often, one line runs across both eyes, framing them like a mask.

Did you know?

Rattlesnakes are born without rattles; they have to shed their skin 2–3 times before they are able to rattle. The striking distance of a prairie rattlesnake is two-thirds the length of its body. The prairie rattlesnake has the largest range of any rattlesnake species in the country. They are mostly diurnal but become nocturnal during extreme heat.

Most Active   Hibernates

Note: Prairie rattlesnakes are venomous (toxic). If you see one, observe or admire it from a safe distance.

Prairie Rattlesnake

Crotalus viridis

Size: 36–60 inches long; weighs 8–13 ounces

Habitat: Prairies, grasslands, forests, wooded mountains, caves, sandhills, burrows, rock ledges, and alongside streams

Range: Canada south to Texas and Mexico. Range extends over the Great Plains into Iowa, Colorado, and Idaho, as well as several other states. In Colorado, they are found throughout most of the state except for a few central counties.

Food: Owls, other snakes, birds, smaller amphibians and reptiles, and small mammals like prairie dogs, squirrels, rabbits, and voles

Mating: Midsummer and early fall. Males seek out females to mate with.

Nest: They will utilize abandoned burrows from prairie dogs and other rodents.

Eggs: No eggs; give live birth

Young: Give birth to up to 25 young, depending on size of female. Young may be born 3–4 months after mating. They do not receive any parental care and reach maturity between 3–5 years.

Predators: Golden eagles, hawks, roadrunners, and other snakes

Adult prairie or Great Plains rattlesnakes have a triangular head, narrow neck, and a thick body. They have a blunt nose with heat-seeking pits on either side of it. Their body is various shades of light brown, dusty olive, brownish green, and yellow. They have brown or black blotches along their backs. Their underside is cream to light yellow. Younger rattlesnakes are often brighter in color than adult rattlesnakes.

Did you know?
Smooth green snakes will camouflage themselves by moving their head to mimic or copy plants swaying in the wind. There is another species of green snake that can be found in the eastern United States called the rough green snake; it has rough or keeled scales and is more arboreal (or likes to be in trees and off the ground), whereas the smooth green snake prefers to be on the ground, or terrestrial.

Most Active   Hibernates

Smooth Green Snake

Opheodrys vernalis

Size: 2–2½ feet long; weighs ¹⁄₁₀ ounce

Habitat: Shrublands, prairies, grasslands, mountainous areas, meadows, and forests

Range: They are found from southern Canada down into Illinois and a few states in the Midwest and northeastern United States; in western North America, they are found in Texas, Missouri, Colorado, and northern Mexico. They can be found throughout central and western Colorado.

Food: Spiders and other invertebrates

Mating: April and May

Nest: Will lay eggs in a burrow, under rocks, leaves, or in rotting logs. Sometimes have communal nesting sites

Eggs: Up to 13 eggs can be laid, but usually 4-6 oval-shaped white eggs about 1 inch long are laid per clutch

Young: 4-30 days after eggs are laid, snakelets hatch. Hatchlings are 4-6 inches long. They do not receive care from parents at birth. Snakes reach full maturity at around 2 years.

Predators: Birds of prey, mammals, and other snakes

The smooth green snake is a small, skinny, nonvenomous snake with smooth scales. The dorsal or backside is green, and the ventral or underside is whiteish to pale yellow. Young are brownish or gray at hatching and turn green as they age. Females are larger than males. They are most active during the day. They all have round, black eyes.

Did you know?

The snapping turtle's sex is determined by the temperature of the nest! Nest temperatures that are 67–68 degrees produce females, temperatures in the range between 70 and 72 degrees produce both males and females, and nests that are 73–75 degrees will usually produce all males.

Most Active

Snapping Turtle, Common

Chelydra serpentina

Size: 8–16 inches long; weighs 10–35 pounds

Habitat: Rivers, marshes, and lakes; can be found in areas that have brackish water (freshwater and saltwater mixture)

Range: They are found throughout the Eastern portion of the state of Colorado; also found in the eastern US and southern Canada.

Food: These omnivores (eat both plants and animals) eat frogs, reptiles, snakes, birds, small mammals, and plants.

Mating: April–November are the breeding months; lays eggs during June and July

Nest: Females dig a hole in sandy soil and lay the eggs into it.

Eggs: 25–42 eggs, sometimes as many as 80 or more

Young: Like sea turtles, snapping turtles have temperature-dependent sex determination (TSD), meaning the temperature of the nest determines the sex of the young. Hatchlings leave the nest between August and October. In the North, turtles mature at around 15–20 years, while southern turtles mature around 12 years old.

Predators: Raccoons, skunks, crows, dogs, and humans

The snapping turtle's carapace (top shell) is dark green to brown and usually covered in algae or moss. The plastron (or bottom of the shell) is smaller than the carapace. They are crepuscular animals that are mostly active during the dawn and dusk hours. Young turtles will actively look for food. As adults, they rely heavily on ambushing to hunt; they bury themselves in the sand with just the tip of their nose and eyes showing.

Did you Know?

Speckled kingsnakes are also called the "salt-and-pepper snakes." They get their name due to their large size and the fact that they eat snakes that are not only longer than them, but also those that are venomous. They have some immunity to (can't get hurt by) venom.

Most Active

Hibernates

Speckled Kingsnake
Lampropeltis holbrooki

Size: 36–48 inches long; can reach up to 72 inches; weighs 3–5 pounds

Habitat: City areas, wetlands, grasslands, woodlands, forests, floodplains, fields near streams, shrublands, and shortgrass prairies

Range: They can be found from Iowa to states of the Gulf Coast and west from Texas to eastern New Mexico, Colorado, and throughout most of Kansas. In Colorado, they can be found in the southeastern corner of the state.

Food: They are carnivores that eat rodents, birds, lizards, snakes, eggs, and amphibians.

Mating: Breed in spring once they come out of hibernation

Nest: No nest; they lay eggs under rocks, stumps, logs, or dying plant materials.

Eggs: 6–23 eggs are laid at a time.

Young: Snakelets hatch 8–12 weeks after laying. They are 7–9 inches long and reach adulthood 4–6 months after hatching.

Predators: Red-tailed hawks, pet cats, great horned owls, golden eagles, and other snakes, including other speckled kingsnakes

Speckled kingsnakes are nonvenomous snakes that have smooth scales. They have black eyes and a yellow underside with irregular black barring across the body. Their topside has a black head, body, and tail. Each black scale has a yellow spot at the front toward the center of the scale. Sometimes, the yellow spots will fuse together and form bars on the back. Males are just a little longer than females.

Did you know?

Spiny softshell turtles will bury themselves under a layer of mud at the bottom of a lake, with only their head sticking out, and catch prey as it passes by. In addition to breathing through their lungs, they can extract oxygen from the water through their skin; this aids them in being able to stay underwater for over 4 hours.

Most Active

Spiny Softshell Turtle

Apalone spinifera

Size: Female: 7–19 inches long (carapace); males: 5–10 inches long; females weigh 20–30 pounds, while males are considerably smaller.

Habitat: Sand bars, lakes, rivers, wetlands, and city areas

Range: In North America, they can be found as far north as Canada and as far south as Mexico. They can be found in South Carolina and Georgia and as far west as California. In Colorado, they can be seen in eastern and central areas of the state.

Food: Aquatic insects, fish, snails, tadpoles, and crayfish

Mating: Mating takes place in the spring.

Nest: Eggs are buried in a flask-shaped chamber that is around 4–10 inches deep, along rivers, in sand bars, or on loose soils on banks.

Eggs: 4–38 white eggs are laid per clutch.

Young: Young hatch between 65–85 days after laying. Young turtles are about 1½ inches long at hatchling. While in other turtle species the sex of hatchlings is determined by temperature, in spiny softshell turtles, it is determined by genetics. Females become reproductively mature at around age 8–9, while males become mature at around age 4.

Predators: Raccoons, herons, large fish, and foxes

Spiny softshell turtles are brown-to-olive, flat-shaped turtles with dark spots on their back and limbs. They have a long, snorkel-like nose and webbed feet. The front of the carapace has spines and bumps. Females are larger than males, but males have longer and thicker tails. Their shell is leathery and lacks scutes or scales. The underside, or plastron, is cream or yellow.

Did you know?

Horned lizards are named for the crown of horns on their head. Although sometimes called horned toad, horned frog, or horny toad, they are not amphibians, but reptiles. When threatened, horned lizards will inflate themselves with air to look larger. If this technique doesn't work, they can spray blood from the corners of their eyes, confusing predators and allowing them to escape.

Most Active   Hibernates

Texas Horned Lizard

Phrynosoma cornutum

Size: 2½–4 inches long; weighs 1–3½ ounces

Habitat: Plains, grasslands, open dry areas, prairies, and sandy areas

Range: They are found in the south-central United States to northern Mexico. In Colorado, they can be found in the southeastern part of the state.

Food: Harvester ants make up most of their diet, but they will eat other ants and insects, as well as spiders.

Mating: Mid-April to mid-June after hibernation

Nest: Females dig a nest in loose soil or under large rocks.

Eggs: Females lay 14–37 eggs in late May, June, or July.

Young: Eggs hatch within 1–2 months after laying. They are independent at hatching and will reach reproductive maturity at around 2 years.

Predators: Lizards, ground squirrels, hawks, coyotes, snakes, roadrunners, and pet cats and dogs

Texas horned lizards are small but stocky (wide and flat-bodied). Two rows of enlarged fringed scales run down both sides of their body. Their limbs have pointed scales. They have multiple horns on their head, with two of them longer than the others. Most horned lizards have a light-tan or buffy-colored line that extends down their back. They have two large dark spots behind their head, with more dark markings along their back. Their underside is tan to cream-colored.

Did you know?

The western tiger salamander is the state amphibian of Colorado. They can grow up to 14 inches long and live over 20 years! Western tiger salamanders migrate to their birthplace to breed. Tiger salamanders have a hidden weapon! They produce a poisonous toxin that is secreted or released from two glands in their tail. This toxin makes them taste bad to predators and allows them to escape.

Most Active

Hibernates

Western Tiger Salamander

Ambystoma mavortium

Size: 7–14 inches long; weighs 4½ ounces

Habitat: Woodlands, marshes, and meadows; they spend most of their time underground in burrows.

Range: They are found across much of Colorado; populations are found in the western United States.

Food: They are carnivores that eat insects, frogs, worms, and snails.

Mating: Tiger salamanders leave their burrows to find standing bodies of freshwater. They breed in late winter and early spring after the ground has thawed.

Nest: No nest, but eggs are joined together into one group in a jelly-like sack called an egg mass. An egg mass is attached to grass, leaves, and other plant material at the bottom of a pond.

Eggs: There are 20–100 eggs or more in an egg mass.

Young: Eggs hatch after 2 weeks, and the young are fully aquatic with external gills. Limbs develop shortly after hatching; within 3 months, the young are fully grown but will hang around in a vernal pool. Individuals living in permanent ponds can take up to 6 months to fully develop.

Predators: Young are preyed upon by diving beetles, fish, turtles, and herons. Adults are preyed upon by snakes, owls, and badgers.

Western tiger salamanders have thick black, brown, or grayish bodies with uneven spots of yellow, tan, brown, or green along the head and body. The underside is usually a variation of yellow. Males are usually larger and thicker than females.

Did you know?
Wood frogs are one of the few amphibians found in the Arctic Circle. They can stop their hearts and breathing when hibernating. They have a special antifreeze that keeps their cells from freezing. Eggs are not harmed by freezing; the eggs that are fertilized will stop developing until the weather warms up.

Most Active   Hibernates

Wood Frog

Lithobates sylvaticus

Size: 2–3¼ inches long; weighs ¼ ounce

Habitat: Bogs, meadows, temporary wetlands, forests, marshes, and swamps

Range: Can be found throughout Colorado and the United States as far north as Alaska and as far south as Alabama, with range extending westward into Idaho.

Food: As adults: insects, snails, worms, slugs, and spiders and other arachnids. As tadpoles: vegetation, algae, and decaying plant material

Mating: Early spring in March, sometimes even before ice and snow has started to melt

Nest: No nest; lays eggs in ponds

Eggs: A mass of 1,000–3,000 eggs

Young: Tadpoles hatch 9–30 days after laying. Will turn into frogs in 6–9 weeks and reach reproductive maturity around 1–2 years.

Predators: Snapping turtles, salamanders, raccoons, skunks, beetles, coyotes, foxes, other wood frogs, and birds

Both males and females are brown, dirty red, or tannish in color. They have bumpy skin and a black mask like raccoons or superheroes! They have a pale stomach that is usually yellow to off-white. They have a skin fold that runs down the back from the eyes.

Glossary

Adaptation—An animal's physical (outward) or behavioral (inward) adjustment to changes in the environment.

Amphibian—A small animal with a backbone, has moist skin, and lacks scales. Most amphibians start out as an egg, live at least part of their life in water, and finish life as a land dweller.

Biome—A part or region of Earth that has a particular type of climate and animals and plants that adapted to live in the area.

Bird—A group of animals that all have two legs and feet, a beak, feathers, and wings; while not all birds fly, all birds lay eggs.

Brood—A group of young birds that hatch at the same time and with the same mother.

Carnivore—An animal that primarily eats other animals.

Clutch—The number of eggs an animal lays during one nesting period; an animal can lay more than one clutch each season.

Crepuscular—The hours before sunset or just after sunrise; some animals have adapted to be most active during these low-light times.

Diurnal—During the day; many animals are most active during the daytime.

Ecosystem—A group of animals and plants that interact with each other and the physical area that they live in.

Evolution—A process of change in a species or a group of animals that are all the same kind; evolution happens over several generations or in a group of animals living around the same time; evolution happens through adaptation, or physical and biological changes to better fit the environment over time.

Fledgling—A baby bird that has developed flight feathers and has left the nest.

Gestation—The length of time a developing animal is carried in its mother's womb.

Herbivore—An animal that primarily eats plants.

Hibernate—A survival strategy or process where animals "slow down" and go into a long period of reduced activity to survive winter or seasonal changes; during hibernation, activities like feeding, breathing, and converting food to energy all stop.

Insectivore—An animal whose diet consists of insects.

Incubate—When a bird warms eggs by sitting on them.

Invasive—A nonnative animal that outcompetes native animals in a particular area, harming the environment.

Mammal—An air-breathing, warm-blooded, fur- or hair-covered animal with a backbone. All mammals produce milk and usually give birth to live young.

Migration—When animals move from one area to another. Migration usually occurs seasonally, but it can also happen due to biological processes, such as breeding.

Molt—When animals shed or drop their skin, feathers, or shell.

Nocturnal—At night; many animals are most active at night.

Piscivore—An animal that eats mainly fish.

Predator—An animal that hunts (and eats) other animals.

Raptor—A group of birds that all have a curved beak and sharp talons; they hunt or feed on other animals. Also known as a bird of prey.

Reptile—An egg-laying, air-breathing, cold-blooded animal that has a backbone and skin made of scales, which crawls on its belly or uses stubby legs to get around.

Scat—The waste product that animals release from their bodies; another word for it is poop or droppings.

Talon—The claw on the feet seen on raptors and birds of prey.

Torpor—A form of hibernation in which an animal slows down its breathing and heart rate; torpor ranges from a few hours at a time to a whole day; torpor does not involve a deep sleep.

Checklist

Mammals

- [ ] American Badger
- [ ] American Beaver
- [ ] Bison
- [ ] Black Bear
- [ ] Black-footed Ferret
- [ ] Black-tailed Prairie Dog
- [ ] Coyote
- [ ] Elk
- [ ] Moose
- [ ] Mountain Lion
- [ ] North American Porcupine
- [ ] Northern Raccoon
- [ ] Northern River Otter
- [ ] Pika
- [ ] Pronghorn
- [ ] Ringtail
- [ ] Rocky Mountain Bighorn Sheep
- [ ] Swift Fox
- [ ] Virginia Opossum
- [ ] White-tailed Deer
- [ ] Yellow-bellied Marmot

Birds

- [ ] American Goldfinch
- [ ] Bald Eagle
- [ ] Belted Kingfisher
- [ ] Black-capped Chickadee
- [ ] Brown-capped Rosy-finch
- [ ] Burrowing Owl
- [ ] Canvasback Duck
- [ ] Cinnamon Teal
- [ ] Double-crested Cormorant
- [ ] Dusky Grouse
- [ ] Ferruginous Hawk
- [ ] Golden Eagle
- [ ] Gray Catbird
- [ ] Great Blue Heron
- [ ] Great Horned Owl
- [ ] Hairy/Downy Woodpecker
- [ ] Lark Bunting
- [ ] Lewis's Woodpecker
- [ ] Mallard
- [ ] Mountain Bluebird
- [ ] Mourning Dove

- ☐ Osprey
- ☐ Peregrine Falcon
- ☐ Sandhill Crane
- ☐ Short-eared Owl
- ☐ Western Tanager
- ☐ White-tailed Ptarmigan
- ☐ Wild Turkey
- ☐ Wood Duck

Reptiles and Amphibians

- ☐ Eastern Collared Lizard
- ☐ Eastern Painted Turtle
- ☐ Great Plains Toad
- ☐ Ornate Box Turtle
- ☐ Plains Hognose Snake
- ☐ Prairie Rattlesnake
- ☐ Smooth Green Snake
- ☐ Snapping Turtle, Common
- ☐ Speckled Kingsnake
- ☐ Spiny Softshell Turtle
- ☐ Texas Horned Lizard
- ☐ Western Tiger Salamander
- ☐ Wood Frog

The Art of Conservation®

Featuring two signature programs, The Songbird Art Contest™ and The Fish Art Contest®, the Art of Conservation programs celebrate the arts as a cornerstone to conservation. To enter, youth artists create an original hand-drawn illustration and written essay, story, or poem synthesizing what they have learned. The contests are FREE to enter and open to students in K-12. For program updates, rules, guidelines, and entry forms, visit: www.TheArtofConservation.org

The Fish Art Contest® introduces youth to the wonders of fish, the joy of fishing, and the importance of aquatic conservation. The Fish Art Contest uses art, science, and creative writing to foster connections to the outdoors and inspire the next generation of stewards. Participants are encouraged to use the Fish On! lesson plan, then submit an original, handmade piece of artwork to compete for prizes and international recognition.

The Songbird Art Contest® explores the wonders and species diversity of North American songbirds. Raising awareness and educating the public on bird conservation, the Songbird program builds stewardship, encourages outdoors participation, and promotes the discovery of nature.

Photo Credits

About the Author

Alex Troutman is a wildlife biologist, birder, nature enthusiast, and science communicator from Austell, Georgia. He has a passion for sharing the wonders of nature and introducing the younger generation to the outdoors. He holds both a bachelor's degree and a master's degree in biology from Georgia Southern University (the Real GSU), with a focus in conservation. Because he knows what it feels like to not see individuals who look like you (or come from a similar background) doing the things you enjoy or working in the career that you aspire to be in, Alex makes a point not only to be that representation for the younger generation, but also to make sure that kids have exposure to the careers they are interested in and the diverse scientists working in those careers.

Alex is the co-organizer of several Black in X weeks, including Black Birders Week, Black Mammologists Week, and Black in Marine Science Week. This movement encourages diversity in nature, the celebration of Black individual scientists, awareness of Black nature enthusiasts, and diversity in STEAM fields.

ABOUT ADVENTUREKEEN

We are an independent nature and outdoor activity publisher. Our founding dates back more than 4 years, guided then and now by our love of being in the woods and on the water, by our passion for reading and books, and by the sense of wonder and discovery made possible by spending time recreating outdoors in beautiful places. I is our mission to share that wonder and fun with our readers, especially with those who haven't yet experienced all the physical and mental health benefits that nature and outdoor activity can bring #bewellbeoutdoors